# Sing Into Your Sixties...
# And Beyond!
## A Manual and Anthology
## For Group and Individual Voice Instruction

Sangeetha Rayapati, DMA

Inside View Press
Delaware, Ohio

**Sing Into Your Sixties...
And Beyond!**

Copyright © 2012 by Sangeetha Rayapati and Inside View Press
All rights reserved

No part of this book may be reproduced, stored in a retrieval system, or transmitted by any means, electronic, mechanical, photocopy, recording, or otherwise, without the express written permission from the author and publisher

All images and musical scores contained within this publication are used with permission under license to the author and Inside View Press

First published by Inside View Press, March, 2012

www.VoiceInsideView.com

ISBN: 978-0-9755307-7-1

Printed in the United States of America

## ACKNOWLEDGEMENTS

To me, being a musician and a scholar means being a practitioner of and partner in collaboration. In the case of this project, neither entity has existed alone. I have collaborated with many people to bring this project to fruition and wish to thank each of them for the significant roles they have played in helping me understand and execute the processes of research, implementation, and dissemination of my work. My colleagues at Augustana College, Jayne Rose, Dan Corts, and Karen Aumueller were essential to the initial study that preceded this book, as were my colleagues in the Music Department who allowed me space and time to conduct voice classes and invite the public into our facilities. The administration at Augustana College provided funds for the securing of initial reprint permissions in the anthology as well as a Presidential Research Grant and sabbatical to conduct and compile my research.

I would also like to thank all of the participants in my voice classes who allowed me the freedom to explore teaching and research techniques and provided valuable feedback about their experiences. My hope is that this book gives them the information that they wanted and needed and inspires them toward continued voice study.

A word of thanks also is owed to Scott McCoy, editor of Inside View Press, who saw the potential in this book and invested so much to make it a reality. He is a tremendous example of a teacher/scholar and I feel privileged to have him as editor. Ron Guastafferi, of Synapse Studios, must also be thanked for his diligence and excellent work on the anatomical artwork in this book.

Finally, I must thank my family— my husband, parents, and children— for allowing me the time and freedom to pursue this goal. Without our collaboration as a family, none of this would have been possible. Thank you.

*Sangeetha Rayapati, March 2012*

# Sing Into Your Sixties... And Beyond!

## Table of Contents

| | |
|---|---|
| Introduction | i |
| **Part I** | 1 |
| Fundamental Vocal Principles: Anatomy, Physiology, and Vocal Techniques | |
| **Part II** | 25 |
| Song Anthology | |

### Folk and Traditional Songs without Accompaniment

| | |
|---|---|
| **Aamulla varhain** (Finnish) | 26 |
| **Ajde Jano** (Serbian) | 26 |
| **Alouette, gentil Alouette** (French) | 27 |
| **Iskat me, mamo** (Bulgarian) | 27 |
| **Nuz my sdais krzescijani** (Polish) | 28 |
| **Sikon** (Greek) | 29 |
| **Tin Tin Tini Mini Hanm** (Turkish) | 29 |
| **This Land was made for You and Me** (American, by Woodie Guthrie) | 30 |
| **This Little Light of Mine** (American) | 32 |

### Folk and Traditional Songs with Piano Accompaniment

| | |
|---|---|
| **Auld Lang Syne** (Old Scotch Air) | 34 |
| **The Blue Alsatian** Mountains (Stephen Adams) | 36 |
| **The Last Rose of Summer** (Thomas Moore) | 38 |
| **The Loreley** (F. Silcher) | 40 |
| **Oh dear! What can the matter be?** (Traditional) | 41 |
| **Oh, Shenandoah** (David Horace Davies) | 43 |
| **Sing Ivy** (Traditional, arr. Holst) | 46 |
| **Slumber my Darling** (Stephen Foster) | 49 |
| **The Storm** (John Hullah) | 52 |
| **There's Music in the Air** (George F. Root) | 55 |

### From the Great American Songbook

| | |
|---|---|
| **Ain't Misbehavin** (Thomas "Fats" Waller) | 57 |
| **Cry Me a River** (Arthur Hamilton) | 59 |
| **Don't Get Around Much Anymore** (Duke Ellington) | 63 |
| **My Funny Valentine** (Richard Rogers) | 67 |

### Sacred Solos

| | |
|---|---|
| **Ah, Holy Jesus** (Richard Walters) | 69 |
| **I Wonder as I Wander** (David Horace Davies) | 73 |

| | |
|---|---|
| **The Lord is my Shepherd** (Robert Leaf) | 77 |
| **O Holy Night** (Adolphe Adam) | 82 |
| **Pie Jesu** (Gabriel Fauré) | 93 |
| **Simple Gifts** (David Horace Davies) | 98 |

Sacred Duets & Trios

| | |
|---|---|
| **Befiehl dem Herrn deine Wege!** (Max Reger) | 102 |
| **Commit Thy Ways to the Lord** (Max Reger) | 109 |
| **Jesus Lover of my Soul** (David Horace Davies) | 116 |
| **Laudate Dominum** (Lorenzo Perosi) | 120 |
| **Magnificat** (Peter Benoit) | 123 |
| **Out of Your Sleep Arise and Wake** (R. Mather) | 126 |
| **Puer Natus in Bethlehem** (Josef Rheinberger) | 130 |

Secular Solos

| | |
|---|---|
| **An die Musik**, low key (Franz Schubert) | 140 |
| **An die Musik**, high key (Franz Schubert) | 142 |
| **Finding Home** (Ricky Ian Gordon) | 144 |
| **Three Emily Dickinson Songs** (Charles B. Griffin) | 148 |
|    **Heart! We will forget him!** | 149 |
|    **I felt a Funeral** | 152 |
|    **Because I could not stop for Death** | 157 |
| **Waiting**, low voice (William Campbell) | 165 |
| **Waiting**, high voice (William Campbell) | 168 |
| **What can we poor Females do** (Henry Purcell) | 171 |

Secular Duets & Trios

| | |
|---|---|
| **Erano I capei d'oro** (Alessandro Kirschner) | 174 |
| **Mägdlein auf die Weise gingen** (Anton Rubsenstein) | 182 |
| **My Dearest, My Fairest** (Henry Purcell) | 186 |
| **Wanderers Nachtlied** (Anton Rubenstein) | 196 |

# Part III . . . . . . . . . . . . . . . . . . . . . . . . . . . . 202
Teacher's Guide

| | |
|---|---|
| What is an Aging singer? | 202 |
| What Can Aging Singers do for Voice Teachers and Choir Directors? | 203 |
| What Can Teachers do for Aging Singers? | 203 |
| What Changes do we need to consider? | 204 |
| Coping with Change | 208 |
| How do we Get Started? | 209 |
| First Encounters and Following Up | 214 |
| Conclusion | 215 |
| Works Cited in the text (bibliography) | 216 |

# Index . . . . . . . . . . . . . . . . . . . . . . . . . . . . . 218

# About the Author . . . . . . . . . . . . . . . . . . . . 219

# INTRODUCTION

The spirit of collaboration is powerful. Musicians collaborate with one another to develop performances that satisfy performer and listener. Teachers, it can be argued, collaborate with students to further the learning process. Colleagues collaborate on projects, teaching, and sometimes in endeavors outside of academia. Such was the case several years ago when choral directors approached me with questions about how best to utilize and teach aging voices in their community choirs. They came to me, a voice teacher, for answers to their questions about breathing, vibrato, intonation, and phrasing because their prior training had focused on vocal development of children, adolescents and young adults. Now they needed a clear understanding of the abilities, limitations, and unique needs of aging singers. Unfortunately, some gave up on these singers entirely and asked them to leave their ensembles.

I understood what these choir directors faced and knew the performance standards they maintained, but was also concerned about the potential psychological repercussions of this exclusion of aging singers. As a committed voice teacher who also is a trained Registered Nurse with experience in geriatrics, I believed that these singers were most likely aware of their vocal issues but were unsure of the best steps to maintain or improve their singing. I gave my friends and colleagues basic pedagogic answers to their questions, but wondered what other resources were available.

Significant research on the aging has been completed in the disciplines of laryngology, speech language pathology, and audiology. But I was surprised to find little extant information on teaching the aging singer, despite the fact that a major demographic shift is about to occur in our nation. The document, "Aging in the United States: Past, Present, and Future" presents statistics from the 1990 Census indicating that by 2020 there will be a 74% growth in population ages 65-74 and that one in five Americans will be in this group by 2030 (U.S. Bureau).

After noting this lack of information, I decided that my background in anatomy, physiology, and psychology from my days in nurse's training and my specialization in voice pedagogy in graduate school had prepared me well for undertaking research about teaching techniques for aging singers. In addition to my experience with aging singers both as a conductor and chorister, I had provided voice instruction in group and one-on-one settings. These experiences helped me devise a research project that expanded my understanding of effective teaching methods for older singers in solo and choral situations.

My inquiries began through interdisciplinary study with colleagues at Augustana College; their expertise informed my study design and implementation. Jayne Rose, Dan Corts, Karen Aumueller, and Donald Shaw helped me examine physiologic changes to the lungs and larynx, and assess life satisfaction. The experiment consisted of pre- and post-study measurements of these areas, ten weeks of voice class (one per week), and analysis of the results. Through a later, qualitative analysis, I discovered that the techniques participants had learned improved both their vocalism and their personal satisfaction from musical activities.

I asked the singers in my study to keep anonymous journals, in which they recorded the things they learned, their reactions to the class and whether or not they felt their singing was improving. These journals, supported by my observations of their sound, provided strong evidence of the success I was having in helping our sample population to sing well. I came to the conclusion that voice class was an effective approach to training aging singers—students improved and stayed motivated to learn. I also believed that many of the techniques I used in that class situation could be transferred to a choral rehearsal. The information gleaned from that research and from its comparison with existing information is the foundation of *Sing Into Your Sixties... And Beyond!*

I believe that teachers and choir directors are called not only to create art, but also to serve; therefore, we must supply ourselves with relevant information that makes genuine and effective service possible. Whether we teach individuals or groups, we provide outlets for musical expression for singers of all ages. In doing so, we must maintain acceptable musical standards if we are to ensure the relevance of our craft for future generations. By doing this we promote music as a subject and tool for lifelong learning.

We must be ready and willing to combat our cultural stereotypes about aging, and instead, seek to enhance each other's lives through music. The remainder of this book will detail psychosocial, cognitive, anatomic, and physiologic considerations for teaching older adults, helping to empower voice-teaching professionals for service to this growing demographic.

# Part I

# Fundamental Vocal Principles: Anatomy, Physiology, and Vocal Techniques

The voice is an amazing instrument. Without valves or keys we can make innumerable sounds over a wide range of pitch and loudness. We can sing in different styles and change the brilliance of our tone almost instantaneously. This flexibility is wonderful but can also be a source of frustration, especially when we sing without truly understanding our instrument.

Knowing how our voices function is essential to diagnosing problems and improving our singing abilities. However, too much detailed information can confuse us and make us feel helpless. This section will introduce you to each step in the process of singing and provide exercises for focused study and integration of skills.

The initial impetus for singing begins in our brain. Once we decide that we're going to sing, it sends messages to the rest of the body to initiate respiration (breathing), phonation (making sound), resonation (amplifying sound), and articulation (shaping sounds into words).

## Respiration

The primary structures of the respiratory system involved in singing are the larynx, trachea, bronchioles, bronchi, lungs and diaphragm. Musculoskeletal structures also are involved in breathing, such as the internal and external intercostal muscles that lift and lower the ribcage for inhalation and exhalation (see Figure 1). As part of the respiratory system, the larynx functions as the entrance and exit of the airway. The **trachea** is responsible for directing air to and from the **bronchi** and **bronchioles** where blood gasses are exchanged.

The **lungs**, of course, are the organs that make the exchange of air possible, and the **diaphragm**, a large dome-shaped muscle that separates our thoracic and abdominal cavities, is responsible for balancing air pressures within the chest. It descends on inhalation and ascends on exhalation. In singing, our goal is to maintain balanced tension between the muscles of the abdomen and ribcage so that we can sing effortlessly. If we are too stiff and straight we can create tension; but if we hunch over, no room is provided for expansion of the ribcage or belly.

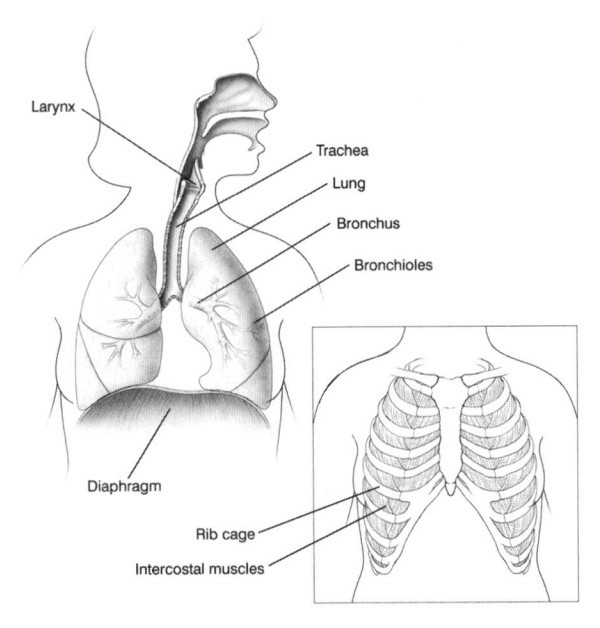

**Figure 1: Respiratory System**

Posture and muscle interactions have the biggest impact on this balance. In this way we maximize the use of air we have inhaled and increase our ability to sing longer phrases.

The thing to remember is that we must release all muscle tension in the lower abdominal muscles to allow the diaphragm to drop and draw air into the lungs. We also must expand our ribcages to allow for the best breath energy, but this can't be done with a stiff posture. Therefore, a free and flexible body allows for the optimal energized release of air for phonation.

## Age-related Changes

In an aging respiratory system there can be malfunctions in any of these component parts (muscles, skeletal framework, air exchange). Generally, diaphragm strength is reduced, meaning that it must work harder to remain in a descended position or, because of an increase in respiratory rate, it is working harder during each cycle of breathing. This elevation in respiratory work can lead to increased overall fatigue, which can translate to sub-par vocal tone, phrasing, and tuning.

Changes in the lungs also lead to a similar increase in demand on the respiratory system. Lung tissue loses elasticity, making it more difficult for the lungs to fill and empty (Berk 569). Added to this are changes in lung volumes, which play a role in both musical phrasing and breath support. Residual volume, the air left over after expiration, increases and "undermines primary respiratory improvements learned in earlier voice training. This can lead to hyperventilation" (Sataloff, Spiegel & Rosen 129). Vital capacity, the amount of air we can take into the lungs, decreases as well, and we find it harder to manage our breathing. In addition, the cartilages that aid in the process of lifting and lowering the ribs during inhalation and exhalation start to stiffen, decreasing the range of motion of the ribs and making it more difficult to inhale (Digiovanna 84). A barrel chest also may form, meaning that the chest becomes "deeper front to back" and makes "deep inspiration" difficult (Digiovanna 85). The efficiency of inhalation, air exchange, and exhalation are all affected by changes in the component parts of the respiratory

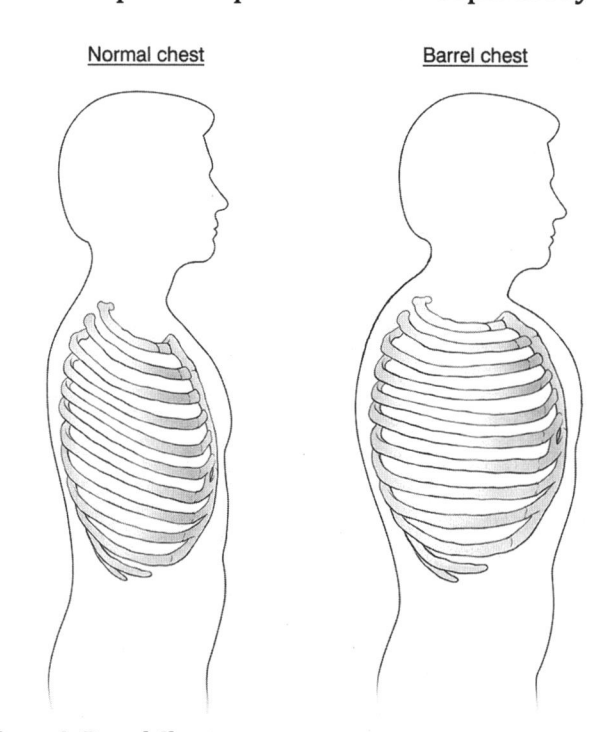

**Figure 2: Barrel Chest**

system. Most of these changes lead to difficulty with breathing and therefore with phrasing and vocal tone quality.

Another factor affecting breath support and tone quality is fat deposits. These deposits increase as we age (in the lower torso for women and upper torso for men), causing the body to work harder to move this larger body mass during inhalation (Berk 502). The generalized atrophy of fast-twitch muscle fibers in the body can lead to a loss of speed and strength, which in turn leads to breathing difficulties and compensation with excess neck and tongue tension (Berk 571; Sataloff, Spiegel and Rosen 129).

**Exercises for Improving Respiration**

The following exercises focus on developing coordination of the muscles used for breathing. They require you to energize exhalation more strongly than actually is needed for optimal phonation; this exaggeration will help you become more comfortable with the physicality of breathing independent of the songs you sing. We isolate the components of the singing process to master them individually before they are integrated into a balanced whole.

1. **Muscular Awareness**. There are several ways to become oriented to these low muscles in your torso, both in your front and your back. One way is to stand and find the fleshy area between your lowest rib and your hips. Place your hands

there with your thumbs in front and your middle fingers touching in the back. Bend over from your hips, elongating your spine, and take a deep breath in. What happens to your middle fingers? Do they stay together? Pull apart? *They should pull apart when you take that deep breath.* What happens to your belly? Does it fall toward the floor? *It should fall away from you to the floor.*

2. **Mirror image**. Imagine you are looking at your side profile in a mirror while contracting your abdominal muscles to flatten your tummy. Next, release those muscles you just held tightly. These are the muscles you will continue to manipulate as you balance respiration with phonation and resonance. Many people call this breath support; I call it the gut tug. This action simply is the force that balances all of the muscular energies that play a part in creating a tension-free, balanced tone. To further explore this power, stand in a leaning-forward position at a 45 or 50 degree angle to the floor. Pull in those same muscles you used above, and then let them drop toward the floor by releasing all tension. Gradually take yourself to a standing position and see if you can maintain the same control over your abdominal muscles.

3. **Dog pant**. Stand in a balanced position and let your tongue hang out. Try to imitate a dog panting by quickly pulling in your abdominal muscles and letting them relax outward again with each breath. Notice how your abdominal area moves in and out very quickly. Try slowing down and speeding up your pace, developing control over your abdominal muscles as you go.

4. **Movement.** Try briskly walking around your practice space or walking up and down several stairs. When you feel slightly out of breath, stop and notice how your abdomen is moving. When you sing your next exercise, use these muscles to help you inhale and exhale.

5. **Pulsations**. Use your abdomen to pulsate on an [s], [sh] or [f] five times. Deliberately, but gently, pull your abdominal wall inward with each consonant sound. As you become better coordinated, increase your speed or number of pulsations from five to seven or nine before taking a breath again. This motion is similar to what you do during

singing and is good way to train your muscles.

6. **Staccato**. This exercise requires your abdominal muscles to pulsate, much like they did in exercise five, but with less exaggerated effort. On a syllable such as [ha], sing a vocal warm-up (vocalise) in a staccato or separated style. It could be the outline of a chord (arpeggio), the first five notes of a scale, or anything you make up on your own. Make sure your abdomen pulses IN on the syllable and releases OUT on the rest between.

7. **Brrr/Sniff**. Practice buzzing your lips. If you have trouble sustaining this sound, lightly place your index fingers on the sides of your lips and blow, pretending you're saying, "brrr, it's cold outside." Sing the following pattern, inhaling and releasing your abdominal muscles after each group of two pitches and pulling in with them during each group. Again, this exaggerated abdominal motion helps to train your abdominal muscles, but should not be used to the same extent while singing. It also is one of the first exercises you might do that requires you to sustain pitch while moving muscles. Sustaining the pitch on a "brrr" is a very relaxing, healthy vocalise.

8. **"Chicken" walk**. To loosen inhibitions, do something silly—the chicken walk. Bend at your knees and keep your torso upright. You should feel a moderate amount of tension in your thighs and possibly some in your low abdominal muscles as you work to stay upright. Try to maintain this position while walking around the room. You might feel silly, but your body will be getting used to a lower center of balance, which will help you avoid breathing with tension in your upper body.

## Other ideas

- Use props to help you get a sense of how your air is supposed to move. For example, use a pinwheel and try to make it turn steadily with the energy of your breath. This is the breath energy used to sing a phrase really loudly (fortissimo air).
- Imagine blowing out lots of candles on a birthday cake.
- With a partner, lean into each other as you sing a phrase. Use enough breath energy to ensure you won't be pushed over by your partner as she pushes back against you.

## Additional Exercises for Orientation and Connecting to Breath

(note: the syllable [ja] used in these vocal exercises is the common phonetic notation for [ya])

**1.**

ja ja ja ja ja ja ja_____
ha ha ha ha ha ha ha_____

**2.**

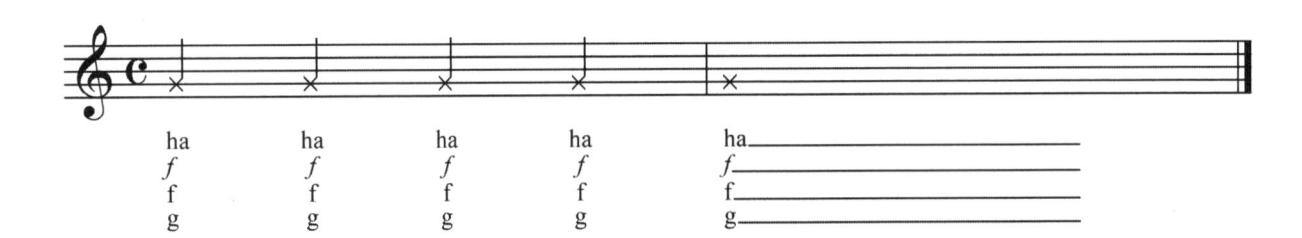

ha ha ha ha ha_____
$f$ $f$ $f$ $f$ $f$_____
f f f f f_____
g g g g g_____

**3.**

mja a a a a_____

**4.**

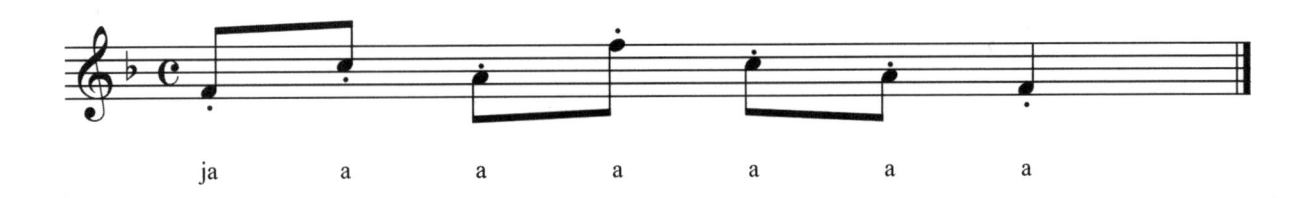

ja a a a a a a

Exercise four also can be sung legato.

*[musical notation with syllable "ja"]*

5.

*[musical notation with dynamic markings "f"]*

## Phonation

The curious teacher and student will find excellent resources with detailed information on the laryngeal mechanism and how it works to make sound (**phonation**) in speech pathology and most voice pedagogy textbooks. A simplified approach is appropriate here. As Clifton Ware states, the basic framework of the larynx consists of a bone and three cartilages—the **hyoid bone** at the top of the larynx, the **thyroid cartilage** or "Adam's Apple," and the **cricoid cartilage**, the base of the larynx that connects with the trachea (Ware 97). Above this structure is the **epiglottis,** which protects the airway from food or other materials that are swallowed. Inside this basic laryngeal framework are the **arytenoid cartilages**, two pyramidal structures that are responsible for

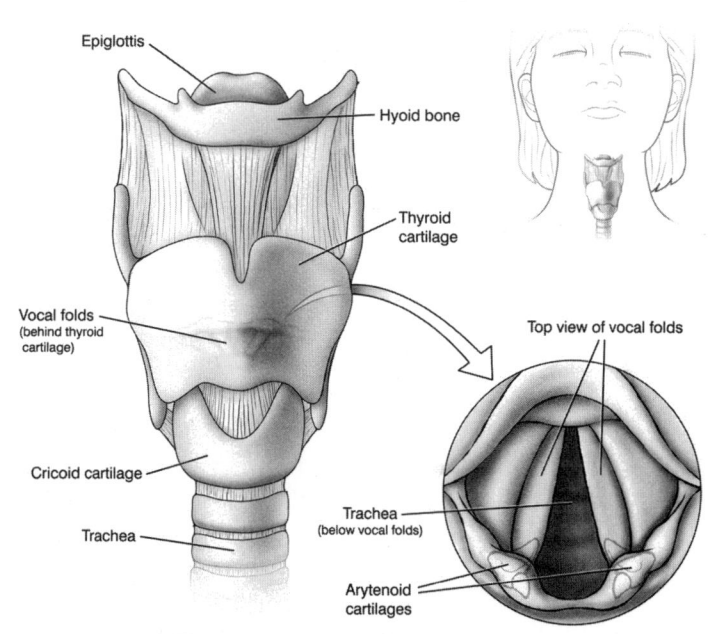

**Figure 3: Larynx and Vocal Folds**

bringing the vocal folds together and pulling them apart (processes known as adduction and abduction). Membranes and ligaments connect these cartilages together to form one functioning unit in which the vocal folds vibrate to create sound. The **vocal folds** (sometimes less accurately called the vocal cords) consist of 3 main parts: the body, transition, and cover. The **body** is comprised of the **vocalis muscle,** also known as the **thyroarytenoid muscle**, which can be compared to a stiff bundle of rubber bands. The transition layer, called the **lamina propria**, includes two layers of collagenous fibers and a middle layer of more elastic fibers.

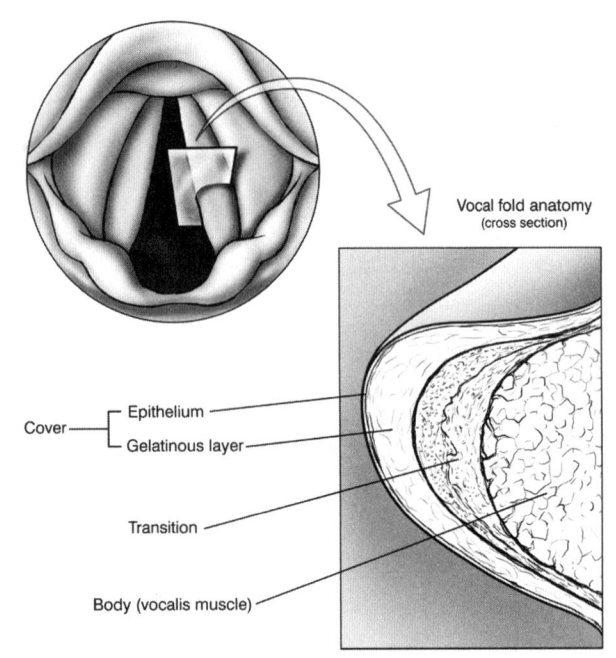

**Figure 4: Structure of Vocal Folds**

Running through the lamina propria is the semi-stretchable **vocal ligament**, which prevents the folds from being strained through excess elongation when singing high notes. The **cover** is a gelatinous layer plus an outer skin, or **epithelium** (Ware 99). This is the layer that protects the folds, especially when proper hydration is maintained (see Figure 4). Air passing between the vocal folds—an area known as the **glottis**—causes them to open and close very rapidly, an action known as oscillation. This happens over a thousand times a second when a woman sings high C ($C^6$)! The oscillating vocal folds chop into and periodically interrupt the moving airstream, which is what makes sound. When healthy, the vocal folds are extremely flexible and strong, enabling great versatility in the singing voice. When damaged by poor vocal habits or when compromised by the aging process, they can impair tone quality.

## Age-related Changes

The goal of singing is to achieve a clear even tone that is easily produced throughout one's range. Tense and breathy sounds are evidence of malfunction, unless purposely used in a particular style of music. This concept is known as **timbre** or tone quality. Sound can be described as breathy, unsupported, brusque, and sometimes stiff. Beyond that, many observers note imprecise tuning, excessive **vibrato** (a natural, rhythmic undulation of pitch and loudness), and general difficulty phonating as problems. Although changes in phonation are not age specific—they are more related to physiologic age than chronological age—they can be significant (Sataloff, Spiegel & Rosen 127). Many times problems with phonation are related to respiratory problems and are not isolated in the larynx. For instance, if the lungs or respiratory system cannot provide adequate air pressure, efficient vocal production will suffer (Linville 205). There are, however, significant changes in the laryngeal mechanism that warrant detailed discussion.

Two areas of the laryngeal mechanism encounter major changes during the aging process—muscles, such as those described above, and cartilages. Muscle fiber bundles relax, especially those in the vocalis muscle, which can cause incomplete closure of the glottis and a weak, breathy tone. This relaxation of fibers can take the form of **vocal fold bowing**, which presents as "spindle-shaped gap of varying degrees anteriorly [toward the front] in the glottis" (Linville 206) (Figure 5). Bowing is also described as being caused by a loss of elasticity in, or atrophy of the vocal ligament, which leads to poor glottal closure (Benninger et al 274, Titze 184).

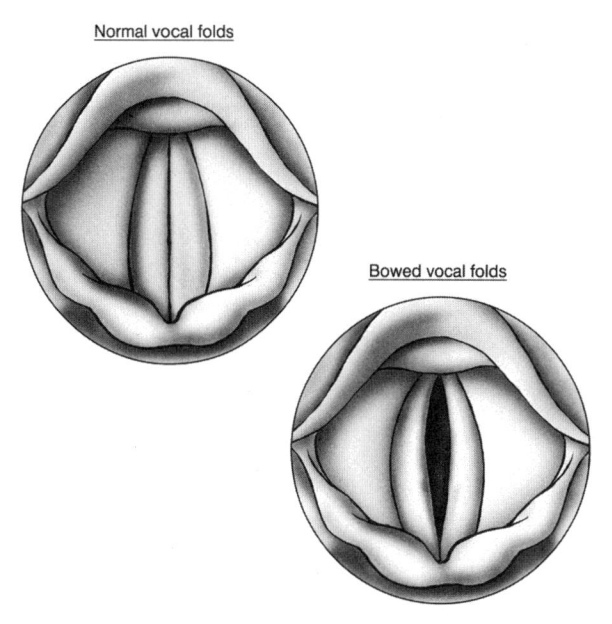

**Figure 5: Normal and Bowed Vocal Folds**

Many changes in the larynx are focused on losses of elasticity and changes to the structure of the larynx. The vocal folds may thin and stiffen because of a loss of collagen and elastin fibers. A roughening of vocal fold edges also might occur, which leads to stiffness and general voice changes (Sataloff, Spiegel & Rosen 128, 130). In addition to this degeneration of muscle tissue, the aging larynx might replace this tissue with connective tissue, which leads to slower muscular contraction (Benninger et al 272).

The layers of the vocal folds themselves also can thicken and the mucosal or outermost layer can lose hydration. Sometimes this thickening and drying is caused by hormonal changes, such as those experienced during and after menopause (Linville 41 and 258). The results are tone quality that might be breathy, coarse, and have a lowered **tessitura** (the area of pitches that are the most comfortable to sing), and decreased pitch range. This is the reason that many older female singers find themselves singing a lower voice part in choir than they did previously.

Sue Ellen Linville confirms this change in comfortable pitch range by explaining that the upper and lower limits of the fundamental frequency (the number of vibrations per second, which is synonymous with pitch) are affected by changes in both the larynx and the respiratory system. As was previously noted, the fundamental frequency is stable in adult females, but hormonal changes in menopause can cause it to drop about 10-15 Herz, or about the musical interval of a whole step (Linville 170). The result is a lowered speaking (and singing) range.

The opposite is true, however, for adult males. A male's speaking fundamental frequency drops in young adulthood but in later life rises about 35 Hz, which can be a major third or more (Linville 172). Linville claims that the cause of this change is muscle atrophy, and/or stiffness of the vocal folds (Linville 172).

The changes already described are by no means the only ones possible. There can be alterations to the laryngeal cartilages, such as ossification, a gradual change from cartilage to bone, which can lead to increased stiffness in the vocal mechanism and an unstable tone; the folds can't come together easily and instead, create a breathy tone (Benninger et al 272). There also may be changes in the articulating surface of the joints between these cartilages that do not allow the vocal folds to close cleanly or completely, which can lead to inaccurate intonation (Benninger et al 272).

Singers might compensate for these changes by increasing laryngeal tension to create sufficient resistance to airflow, which in turn can lead to a pressed (tight or squeezed) vocal quality (Linville 41). In addition, the larynx might descend, causing lowered pitch levels, especially in women (Sataloff, Spiegel & Rosen 130). This manifests itself in ways familiar to choir directors and voice teachers; a singer who had no trouble in the soprano section of the choir now finds the alto section more comfortable.

One also might hear vibrato problems in singers as their voices age. The most comprehensive discussion of vibrato can be located in the text *Vibrato*, by Dejonckere, Hirano and Sundberg. This compilation of studies by various researchers examines vibrato and the history of vibrato, providing some insight into this particularly troublesome issue for aging singers. According to Carl Seashore, vibrato can be defined in several ways, including physically, psychologically, and acoustically. The physical definition is a regular fluctuation in pitch, timbre (color), and/or loudness, while the psychological definition refers to the aesthetics of this pitch fluctuation.

What do listeners consider to be a good or bad vibrato? Is it the same in every culture? Our evidence would say "no." The slow vibrato of traditional Chinese opera is not aesthetically pleasing if used in the classical European opera tradition. Regardless of aesthetic impact, vibrato most likely is created physiologically by bursts of activity in the cricothyroid muscles (qtd. in Davis, 30, 3).

There appear to be many variables at play with troublesome vibrato rates and extent (the range of pitch change). The first major impediment is the slackening of neuromuscular control and tiring of the musculature of the larynx (Hirano 30). The larynx moves with less flexibility to accommodate air pressure and pitch. Secondly, the female larynx lowers during the aging process, which can lead to stronger laryngeal oscillations (periodic movement during phonation) and larger fluctuations in pitch and intensity within vibrato. This action is thought to help combat tightness and rigidity in the vocal mechanism. But when coupled with decreased neuromuscular function, it can lead to the slow undulating vibrato known as "wobble." Reinders states that wobble can be disguised or repaired by an "intelligent management of airflow (142). Exercises for such management methods follow.

These problems are a double-edged sword for singers who encounter them. At times, their voices may sound breathy, so they compensate by stiffening and tightening, a physical state that the mechanism tries to overcome by relaxing with a large vibrato. In addition to the auditory cues to this change, we can be attentive to visual signals from our singers. For example, excess tension in the base of the tongue might manifest in a "wagging" tongue that is synchronized with oscillations of vibrato (Hirano 30). This kind of tension sometimes is referred to as hyperfunction, a state that researcher Gu Li-de states "can create slow undulating vibratos" (146).

**Exercises for Managing Vibrato**

1. Visualize the air coming out in a straight line to avoid excess vibrato. Other techniques include thinking of the air like a fan whose projection is never interrupted by someone walking in front of it.

2. Experiment with crescendos and decrescendos (getting louder and getting quieter). You might need to lighten up your vocal approach if your vibrato is too heavy. This will allow your muscles to relax and enables a freely resonant tone quality. If you have a vibrato that is too fast, a **tremolo**, you will need to engage your breath more energetically to help the tone become more stable. Engaging one's breath and being free of inappropriate muscular tension are the crucial steps in correcting vibrato problems.

In addition to muscle, cartilage, and laryngeal position changes, there are changes in the tissues of the vocal mechanism and peripheral systems that can lead to alterations of sound quality. In general, there is both a deterioration of the central nervous system that decreases control of the larynx, and decreased blood supply to the area (Benninger et al 273). Without adequate blood supply, the tissues are not "fed" properly and can atrophy. This weakens the mechanism in general, rendering it less flexible and less likely to improve. The number of glands that supply lubrication to the vocal folds by secreting mucus decreases, and the folds atrophy (Benninger et al 274). This reduction in lubrication can lead to a hoarse or rough sound. Finally, limitations of range can be attributed not only to the descending larynx, but also to arthritis in joints of the vocal mechanism, hormonal changes that lower the fundamental frequency of a woman's speaking voice (loss of estrogen for example), and edema, or swelling in the tissue spaces (Titze 184 and 185).

As one can imagine, changes to parts of the laryngeal structures that assist in the creation of sung and spoken sounds can have a cumulative effect. Seldom is there a change that is an isolated problem, but rather, it lives in relationship with other changes to the mechanism. These relationships lead to a generalized inefficiency of function (Linville 45) and varying degrees of frustration for people who must cope with these changes. Because the amount and rates of change vary by person (Linville 26), we must be mindful that we address individual needs related to phonation difficulties rather than taking a one-size-fits-all approach.

**Exercises for Improving Phonation**

One of the keys to singing well is connecting your work of breathing to making sound. The following exercises will help you make healthy sounds while balancing them with the proper breath energy.

1. **Pitch levels of speech**: Try saying "Bobby baker bought a bag of bagels" or "Hello, how are you?" in conversational, elevated and sing-song styles, making sure to breathe well before beginning. For example, say a phrase as if you are talking to someone next to you. Next, say a phrase to someone across the street. Finally, experiment with pitch level and breath energy as you play with sound. Remember, you don't want to feel anything in your throat, only your head or face.
2. **Lip flutters**: Use the same bubbling sound you employed in breathing exercise seven (page 5) while singing pitches that slide up and down. Make sure your head does not follow the movement of the pitches.

3. **Slides and glides:** These are some of the most helpful exercises for feeling how easy vocal production is supposed to be. Start at a higher pitch and slide downward on a variety of syllables. Start with [ma], [me] or [mi]. You can progress to [wee], [nu] or [ja].

## Resonation

The third step in the singing process is **resonation**, the natural amplification of sound waves. The benefit of maximizing resonance in the singing voice is that it gives singers the ability to create a balanced, vibrant tone, which is one of the keys to reducing vocal effort and maintaining healthy voice function. Amplification happens when our bodies are well aligned and sound waves can move efficiently. The sound waves are filtered by resonators and shaped by articulators. Resonators in the vocal mechanism include the chest and airways below the glottis, the larynx, pharynx, and mouth (oral cavity), and the nasal and sinus cavities. All of these structures do not work equally to amplify the sound. As a singer you might feel resonance in the chest and head quite a bit, but the hollow structures of the vocal tract (oral cavity, pharynx, and larynx) actually have a larger impact on how others hear your voice. The aging process affects all of these areas.

## Age-related Changes

Changes in resonance can be caused by vocal tract lengthening, laryngeal ptosis (closure of the space), lowered lungs, and a growing facial skeleton, all of which lead to lower resonant frequencies (Linville 179 and 182). These changes not only precipitate alterations in pitch or range, but also usually darken or deepen the tone. A dark or deeper tone is not necessarily problematic, but a vibrant or resonant tone must have brilliance in it as well. If this

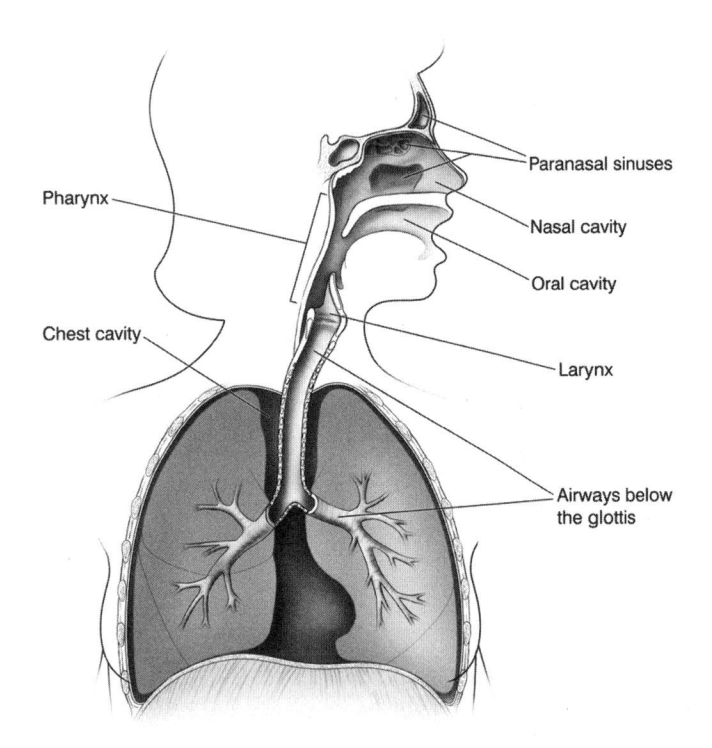

**Figure 6:**
**Resonators and Structures of the Vocal Tract**

bright quality is lacking and the darker tone predominates, accurate tuning may become problematic and pitch range might become more limited.

**Exercises for Improving Resonance**

Exercises for improving resonance are essential for any aging singer. Resonance, when paired with the quality of phonation, can significantly influence development of singing tone that is appropriate for ensemble and solo singing.

1. **Experimentation**: Using a phrase from your music or something simple like, "Hello!", try making nasal sounds (i.e. imitating a witch cackle, Fran Drescher of "The Nanny", or Gilbert Godfrey), and then airy sounds like Marilyn Monroe singing "Happy Birthday, Mr. President" or someone trying to whisper. Finally, try speaking or singing with a well-balanced tone. Notice the differences between these tones, both in sound and sensation. The balanced tone should feel strong but without tension. You should not feel anything in your throat.

2. **Hum/Chew Exercise:** Hum five notes in a descending pattern adding one chewing motion (move the jaw up and down) at the end of each note. Your jaw should start in a relaxed, hanging position, but with your mouth closed and lips touching. You should feel a light buzzing sensation in your face and lips.

3. **Mini-mi/Thiu-Thiu**: Sing a five-note descending pattern with the syllables mini-mi or thiu-thiu on each note. Feel the forward focus toward your forehead or front teeth.

4. **Octave leaps (Di-yo):** Energize the leap between pitches. Sometimes adding physical motion to an exercise can help release tensions. Try bending your knees on the high note if you need to feel more gut tug support or increased freedom. You also could pretend to roll a bowling ball on the high note. The point is that the motion is the opposite of the direction of pitch change. Ask yourself if you are able to maintain that forward resonance that you established in earlier exercises.

*[Musical notation: Di — Yo — Di]*

5. **Arpeggios:** Sing arpeggios in legato, and then staccato fashion. Imagine that you are connecting your air between notes as if you are painting the air in between them. Does your tone feel and sound stable? Do you feel as if you're singing out of your face, or from your throat? *You should be wary of any tensions in the neck and throat, while striving to maintain comfortable focus sensation in the face.*

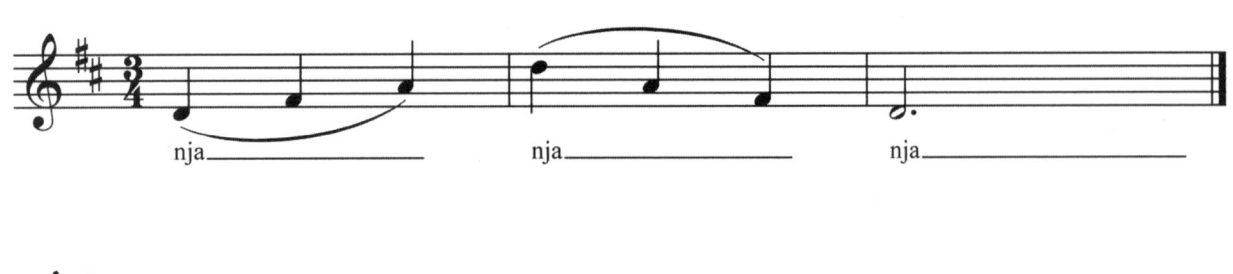

*[Musical notation: nja — nja — nja]*

*[Musical notation: nja — nja — nja]*

6. **Descending Slides:** On a comfortable vowel, sing a descending arpeggio, being sure to slide the pitches between notes in the chord as you go. Keep using your air and tone connection in the balanced fashion you have established. If you feel yourself controlling the sound in your throat, relax and try to refocus on the air or breath.

mjo
da

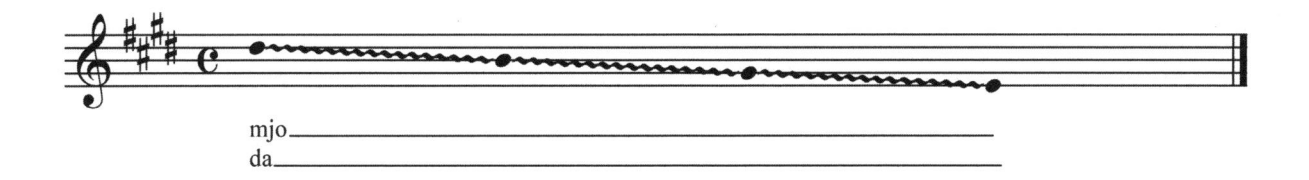

**7. Ner Ner sequence:**

**Step 1**: Sing a five note descending pattern on [ner-ner-ner-ner-ner] as if you are imitating the twang of a banjo being played or the nasality common in some country music singing.

Step 1:
ner   ner   ner   ner   ner

**Step 2**: Sing a five note descending pattern of [ner-a-ner-a-ner], maintaining the nasal quality of step one on the [ner] and opening up on [a].

Step 2:
ner   a   ner   a   ner

**Step 3**: Sing an arpeggio, 1-3-5-8-5-3-1, on the same alternating [ner-a] pattern with a balanced timbre. Try to maintain the forward focus of the nasal exercises, but with open, non-nasal vowels. Do not be afraid to experiment with these sounds. This exercise simply is a means to an end, so don't worry that you are being told to sing with a nasal sound.

Step 3:
ner   a   ner   a   ner   a   ner

## Articulation

The final step in the vocal process is articulation. **Articulation** refers to the shape of a sound as it travels through the vocal tract and is manipulated by the articulators—the lips, tongue, jaw, velum (soft palate), cheeks and larynx. Articulation is the mechanics of producing speech sounds using these articulators (Ware 154). Our goal is for articulators to work freely so that words are clearly understood and the tone is not hindered in any way. We should sound neither shrill nor muddied. In a sense, articulation is about how we make consonant and vowel sounds without compromising the work we've done to establish good breath connection, clean phonation, and balanced resonance.

## Age-related changes

Older singers face particular dilemmas related to this final phase of sound creation. The tongue may move more slowly and with less strength, both of which lead to loss of articulatory precision. When this precision is gone, resonance suffers and we are less able to distinguish vowel sounds. Linville calls this vowel centralization (Linville 182). Because the position of the tongue primarily is responsible for generating vowel sounds, any decline in its effectiveness will make a singer's text less understandable. This is particularly problematic for elderly singers.

It has been documented that tongue strength declines after age 79, and the soft palate becomes less controllable with aging (Linville 47 and 57). While the soft palate is less of a factor in vowel formation, its work with consonant formation might be compromised (i.e. [g], [k], ng]). It also might be a factor that influences the shape of the vocal tract or in the degree of nasality that is present in any particular tone.

There also is evidence in the research literature of decreased articulatory precision of consonants at fast tempos. It might best be understood if one realizes that alterations in how a vowel is produced lead to alterations in both resonance patterns and intelligibility, whereas imprecision in consonant production mostly affects intelligibility (Linville 51). Consonant production also can be affected by changes in the speed of response by oral and facial musculature, which generally become slower because of changes in the central nervous system (innervation).

The breakdown of collagen fibers in facial tissue also can make facial expressions less pronounced. One also must consider additional influences on articulation, such as dentures and other oral appliances. Sataloff, Spiegel, and Rosen (130) note that these can affect articulation, as does **xerostomia,** or dry mouth, which often is experienced by older singers.

**Exercises for Improving Articulation**

Exercises for articulation generally focus on freedom of tongue and jaw movement and flexibility of the soft palate. Paying attention to how consonants are made is a key element in training articulatory mechanisms.

1. **Word Play.** Use the following word combinations to sing the arpeggio with clear, connected vowels. "cool, cool, cool, moon," "pay day today," "fun, fun, in the sun," "sing, sing, please sing," "ta da, ta da.

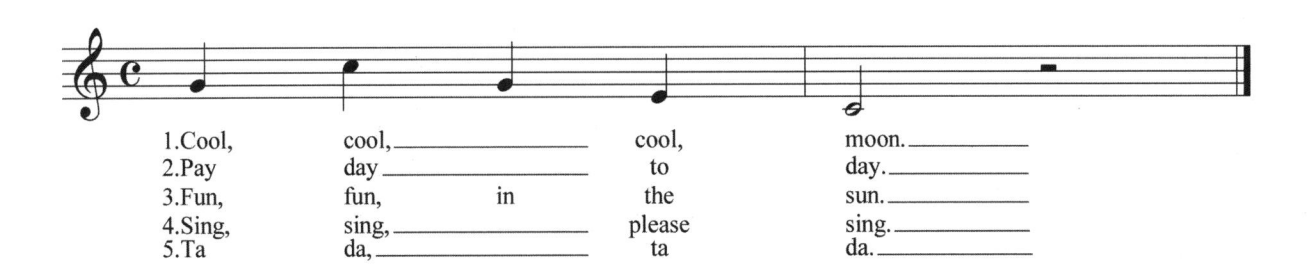

   1. Cool, cool, cool, moon.
   2. Pay day to day.
   3. Fun, fun, in the sun.
   4. Sing, sing, please sing.
   5. Ta da, ta da.

2. **Hung-a:** Use the hung-a exercise to work the muscles of the soft palate. Changing from [ng] to [a] exercises this area, provided the [a] is sung with a non-nasal quality.

   hung a
   hung o
   hung e

3. **Repeated [n]:** Use the [n] of ni-no-ne-na as a voice building consonant. The [n] must be produced with the tongue forward, at the alveolar ridge or the very front of the hard palate, behind the front teeth.

[Musical notation: 3/4 time, with syllables "ni no ne na"]

4. **Alternating Vowels:** Sing combinations of vowel sounds in a pattern of descending skips. Alternate the speed at which you sing this pattern. If you have difficulty at faster speeds, slow down and execute the pattern properly before trying to speed up again.

[Musical notation with vowel syllables: e-a-e-a-e / o-a-o-a-o / i-e-i-e-i]

5. **Tongue flapping:** With your jaw hanging down and the tip of your tongue at the back of your bottom teeth, move the back of your tongue up and down to create a descending [ja] pattern. The jaw needn't move, only the tongue. Use a mirror to check this function or place your finger lightly on your chin to check its movement.

[Musical notation with syllables: ja ja ja ja ja]

## Hearing

The ear and hearing pathways are essential partners in the singing process. Without proper conductivity of sound we cannot adequately hear instructions given by a teacher or conductor and can have difficulty producing the sounds appropriate to the music with which we are engaged. We might misunderstand instructions for pronunciation or create imbalance in the tone of the ensemble as we struggle with filtering out surrounding noise. Before understanding how aging can lead to changes in our hearing processes, we first must understand how we hear, or the hearing pathway.

The hearing pathway consists of five main divisions: the external ear, the middle ear, the inner ear, the hearing nerve (also known as the **auditory** or **cochlear nerve**), and the brain. Sound travels through the air as waves of varying pressure until it arrives at our external ear (**auricle** or **pinna**), where it is funneled by the bony canal (**auditory canal**) to the eardrum (**tympanic membrane**). From the eardrum, the waves are transferred through the middle ear to our inner ear through the vibration of three tiny bones, together known as the **ossicles** and individually as the **malleus, incus,** and **stapes** (hammer, anvil, and stirrups). These vibrations become fluid waves in the **cochlea**, a dense, spiral-shaped, bony capsule, where they displace tiny hair cells called **stereocilia** that line a special membrane within the cochlea (**basilar membrane**). As these hair cells move, they induce a neurochemical reaction that is sent to the brain via the cochlear nerve. In the brain, the neural pathways divide, passing the signals along until they reach the auditory cortex, where they finally are converted into recognizable sound (Antonelli 1-2).

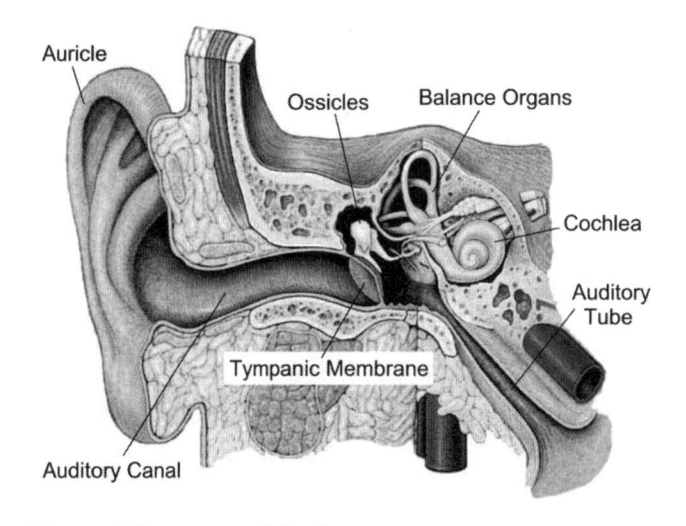

Figure 6: Structures of the Ear

## Age-related changes

The National Institute of Health states that approximately 17 percent of American adults (about 36 million people) say that they have some degree of hearing loss. Roughly one-third of Americans 65 to 74 years of age and 47 percent of those 75 and older have hearing loss (NIH). **Presbycusis**, or age-related hearing loss, is thought to be the most common change to auditory function during the aging process (Huang and Tang 1179). The first manifestation of this type of hearing loss is the inability to hear high-pitched tones, followed by difficulty detecting, identifying, and localizing sounds. Voiceless consonants, such as t, p, k, f, s, and ch, often become difficult to understand, as do some vowel sounds (Huang and Tang 1179).

While there is some debate as to the exact cause of presbycusis, it is well documented that changes to the inner ear are the most common culprits. These changes can include reduced blood supply to the cochlea, reduced nerve conduction from the cochlea, and loss of hair cells that line the basilar membrane, which do not regenerate (Harvard 4). Medical conditions and environmental factors may play the largest roll in these decreases in hearing function.

A sedentary lifestyle that leaves singers susceptible to disease, especially cardiovascular diseases such as high blood pressure, hardening of the arteries, and increased lipid (fat) levels in the blood, are particularly associated with hearing loss. Researchers Hull and Kerschen state: "the cardiovascular system directly influences the viability of the cochlea and the auditory portion of the central nervous system" (10). Other medical conditions that have been linked to an increase in the risk factors for hearing loss include diabetes, immune impairment, and endocrine imbalances. Exposure to cigarette smoke and/or chemical pollutants in the living or working environment also can have negative consequences. But the most common cause of hearing damage by far is chronic exposure to loud sounds. High amplitude soundwaves, whether from a jack hammer, headphones, crowds at a football game, or the trombones in a symphony orchestra, increase one's risk for presbycusis by damaging the hair cells of the inner ear (Huang and Tang 1184).

In addition to the aforementioned causes and risk factors, heredity and gender also appear to be factors in hearing loss. Studies have shown that there is a clear familial link with presbycusis, which is even stronger for female relationships (Huang and Tang 1183). Women have been found to have poorer hearing between the ages of 30 and 80 than men, as well as a greater rate of hearing loss after age 50 (Hull and Kerschen 11).

Symptoms of hearing loss are likely to go unnoticed or unidentified because they slowly creep into one's daily life. Other's speech will sound unclear or background noise will make a conversation difficult to understand, especially at the higher pitch levels associated with women's and children's voices (Harvard 2). Another symptom of hearing loss, **tinnitus,** also common in older people, is a ringing, hissing, or roaring sound in the ears without an external stimulus (Ahmad and Seidman 297). It also can be a symptom of medical conditions, such as allergies and problems in the heart and circulatory system, and can be intermittent, persistent, or stop completely (NIH).

Both tinnitus and age-related hearing loss can be the effect of high sound pressure levels that leave the hair cells of the cochlea in a hyperactive or damaged state, creating a ringing sensation without a stimulus (Ahamad and Seidman 299). The National Institute of Health Senior Health website offers suggestions for questions to ask if you are experiencing tinnitus, or suspect you have hearing loss (NIH):

- Do I have a problem hearing on the telephone?
- Do I have trouble hearing when there is noise in the background?
- Is it hard for me to follow a conversation when two or more people talk at once?
- Do I have to strain to understand a conversation?
- Do people complain that I turn the TV volume up too high?
- Do I hear a ringing, roaring, or hissing sound a lot?
- Do some sounds seem too loud?
- Do many people I talk to seem to mumble or not speak clearly?
- Do I misunderstand what others are saying and respond inappropriately?
- Do I often ask people to repeat themselves?
- Do I have trouble understanding the speech of women and children?

If the answer to three or more of these questions is "yes," it is a good idea to have your hearing evaluated by an audiologist, otologist, or otolaryngologist (ear nose and throat doctor). Treatment ranges from hearing aids and other specialized amplifiers for the home, to surgery and training in lip reading. Untreated hearing loss can lead to negative consequences, many of which affect one's ability to participate in making music.

## Conclusion

It is clear that core components of singing are balance, brilliance, and ease in voice production. We must always sing with energy and have an understanding of what is happening with each kind of tone we make. Age may be a factor in the production of a high-quality tone, but understanding age-related changes can help combat the negative effects of aging. Rather than leaving the focus of our vocal exercise on isolated parts of the singing mechanism, we must integrate them into the entire singing process. We might also consider consultation with a speech-language pathologist or voice therapist who can use **vocal function exercises** to strengthen the muscles used in singing, which is an effective way to challenge the negative effects of vocal aging (Awan 179, Davis vii).

Physiologic aging is an inevitable process, no matter how much our culture tries to combat it or disavow its existence. Increasing our understanding of our bodies and voices can facilitate working within such changes, and helps to clarify any misconceptions we might have about the aging process in general. It should be remembered that physiologic aging occurs at varying rates and is heavily influenced by overall health status. These two factors alone mean that voice teachers, vocal coaches, and choir conductors must be aware of the circumstances unique to members of their ensembles and studios to address their singing and musical needs in the most appropriate manner.

# SONG ANTHOLOGY

# Aamulla Varhain

Kansanlaulu

**Finnish folk song**
Arr. Tanja Kivi

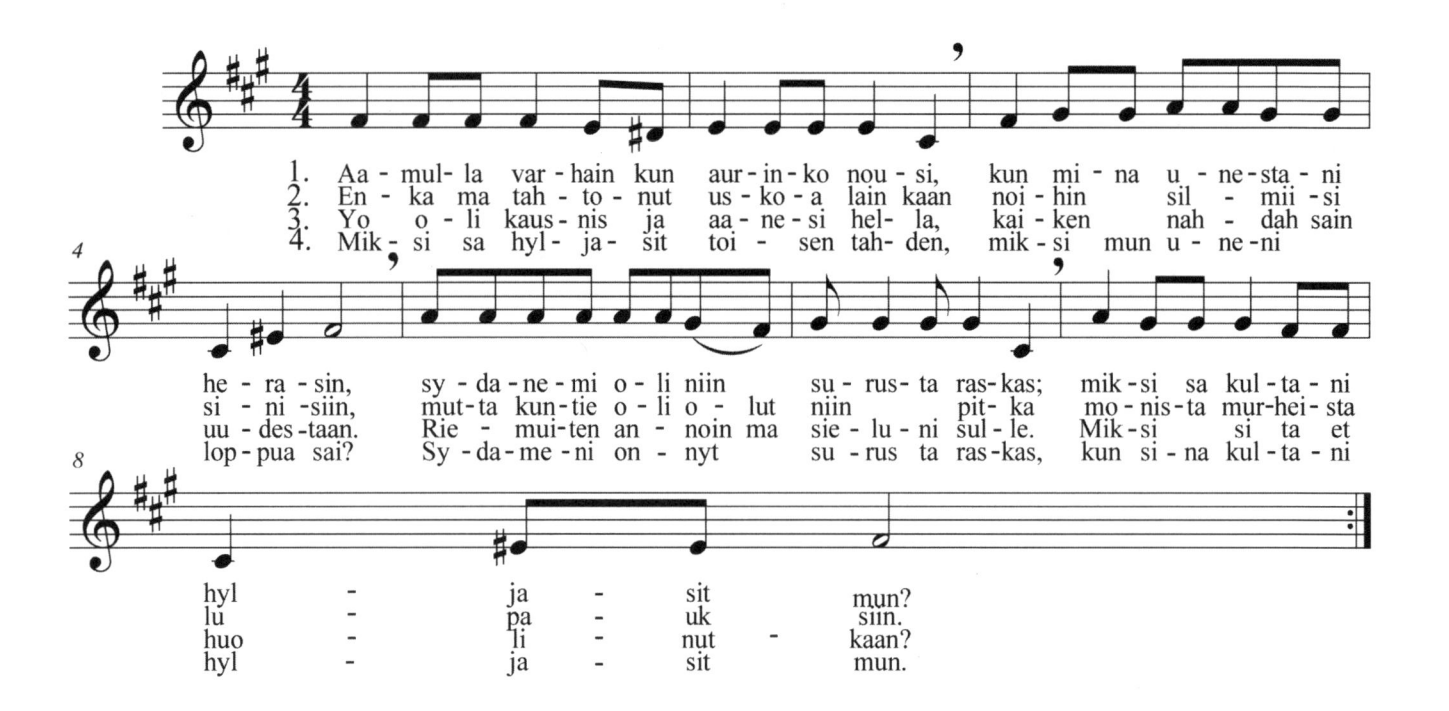

1. Aa-mul-la var-hain kun aur-in-ko nou-si, kun mi-na u-ne-sta-ni he-ra-sin, sy-da-ne-mi o-li niin su-rus-ta ras-kas; mik-si sa kul-ta-ni hyl - ja - sit mun?
2. En-ka ma tah-to-nut us-ko-a lain kaan noi-hin sil-mii-si si-ni-siin, mut-ta kun-tie o-li o-lut niin pit-ka mo-nis-ta mur-hei-sta lu - pa - uk siin.
3. Yo o-li kaus-nis ja aa-ne-si hel-la, kai-ken nah-dah sain uu-des-taan. Rie-mui-ten an-noin ma sie-lu-ni sul-le. Mik-si si ta et huo - li - nut - kaan?
4. Mik-si sa hyl-ja-sit toi-sen tah-den, mik-si mun u-ne-ni lop-pua sai? Sy-da-me-ni on nyt su-rus ta ras-kas, kun si-na kul-ta-ni hyl - ja - sit mun.

# Ajde Jano

Serbia

Music Score
Transcribed By
Lyuben Dossev

Aj-de ja-no ko-lo da ig-ra-mo, Aj-de ja-no, aj-de, du-so, ko-lo da ig-ra-mo;

# Alouette

**French Folk Song**

A-lou-et-te, gen-tille a-lou-et-te, a-lou-et-te, je te plu-me-rai.
je te plu-me-rai la tete, je te plu-me-rai la tete, et la tete, et la tete, et la tete, et la tete,
O! A-lou-et-te, gen tille a-lou-et-te, A-lou-et-te, je te plu-me-rai.

# Iskat me, mamo

Bulgaria

Music Score
Transcribed By
Lyuben Dossev

Is-kat me ma-mo, mo lyat me, zav-rian
zet ma-mo da i-da Da-vat mi, ma-mo da-vat mi,
dva be-li, ma-mo, pe-te-la Dva be-le, ma-mo pe-te-
la, Sus dve cher-ve-ni ko-kosh-ki

# Nuz My Dzis Krzescijani

Anonymous

Nuz my dzis krze sci ja ni, ser decz nie sie
ra duj my dnia dzi siej sze go,
iz sie nim na ro dzil zczy sto sci pa niem skiej Syn bo ga zy we go

# Sikon (Opa Ni Na Nai)
## Greece

*Music Score
Transcribed By
Lyuben Dossev*

Song: Si - ko kho - rep - se kuk - li mu  Na se dho na se kha - ro

tsif - te - te - li tur - ki - ko

Chorus: Ni - na nai yav - rum ni - na nai nai

Ho - pa ni - na ni - na nai, ni - na nai nai  Ni - na nai yav - rum ni - na nai nai

# Tin Tin Tini Mini Hamn
## Turkey

*Music Score
Arranged By
Lyuben Dossev*

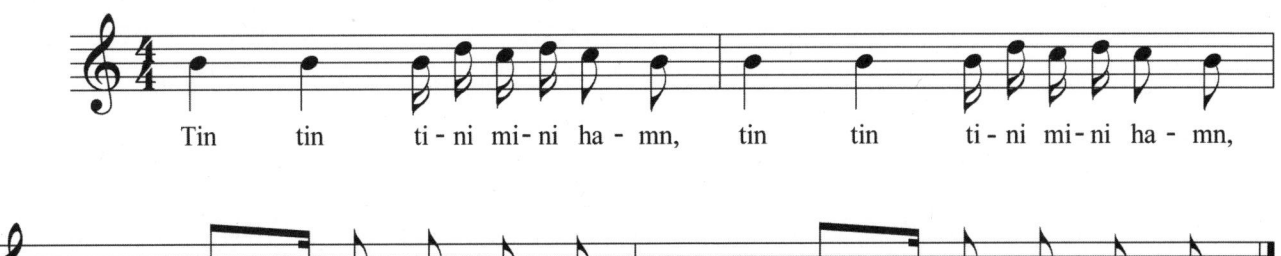

Tin tin ti - ni mi - ni ha - mn, tin tin ti - ni mi - ni ha - mn,

se - ni se - vi - yor ca - mn  se - ni se - vi - yor ca - mn

# This Land Was Made For You And Me

**Woody Guthrie**

This land is your land, this land is my land, from Cal-i-forn-ia, to the New York is-land, from the red-wood for-ests, to the gulf stream wa-ters, this land was made for you and me.

1. As I went walk-ing, that rib-bon of high-way, I looked a-bove me, and saw the Sky-way I looked be-low me, and saw the val-ley this land, was made for you and me. This land is

2. I roamed and ram-bled, and foll-owed my foot-steps, to the spark-ling sands of, her diam-ond des-erts, and all a-round me, a voice was call-ing this land, was made for you and me.

This land is your land, this land is my land, from Cal-i-forn-ia, to the New York is-land,

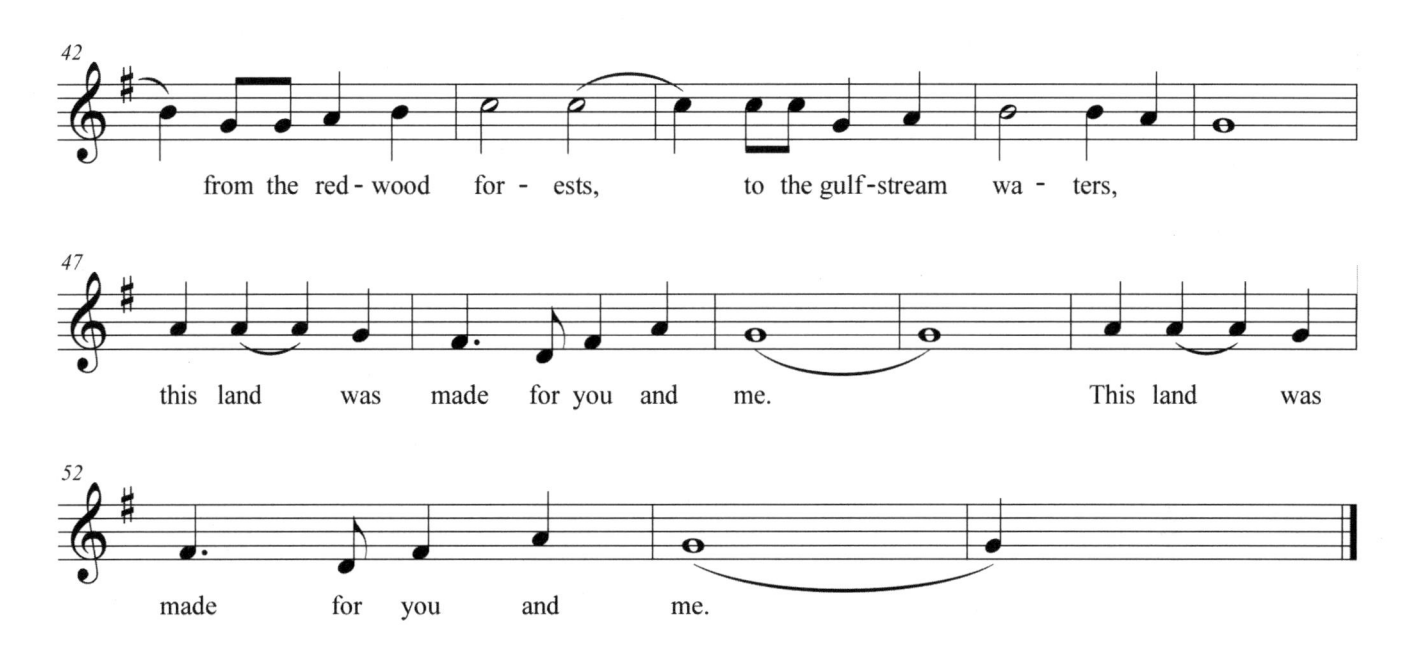

## This Land Was Made For You And Me

from the red-wood for - ests, to the gulf-stream wa - ters,

this land was made for you and me. This land was

made for you and me.

# This Little Light of Mine

**Traditional**
Arr. Consaul

This lit-tle light of mine, I'm gon-na let it shine, oh glo-ry
this lit-tle light of mine, I'm gon-na let it shine, ohhhhhh
this lit-tle light of mine, I'm gon-na let it shine, let it shine
let it shine, shine all o-ver the hea-vens let it shine.

1. Hide it un-der a bush-el "NO!!!" I'm gon-na let it shine,
2. Won't let hat-red reign blow it out, I'm gon-na let it shine,
3. Let it shine til free-dom comes, I'm gon-na let it shine,

oh glo-ry hide it un-der a bush-el "NO!!!" I'm gon-na let it shine,
oh glo-ry won't let hat-red reign blow it out, I'm gon-na let it shine,
oh glo-ry let it shine til free-dom comes, I'm gon-na let it shine,

all o-ver hide it un-der a bush-el "NO!!!" I'm gon-na let it shine,
all o-ver won't let hat-red reign blow it out, I'm gon-na let it shine,
all o-ver let it shine til free-dom comes, I'm gon-na let it shine,

1.
let it shine let it shine, shine all o-ver the heav-ens, let it
let it shine let it shine, shine all o-ver the heav-ens, let it
let it shine let it shine, shine all o-ver the heav-ens, let it

## This Little Light of Mine

shine. / shine. / shine. hea-vens, let it shine let it shine, oh glo-ry

this lit-tle light of mine I'm gon-na let it shine, this lit-tle

light of mine I'm gon-na let it shine, this lit-tle

light of mine, I'm gon-na let it shine, let it shine let it shine,

shine all o-ver the heav-ens, let it shine, oh let it shine.

# Auld Lang Syne

Robert Burns  
♩=60  
Moderato *mf*

Old Scotch Air

Should auld ac-quaint-ance be for-got, and
We twa' ha'e ran a-boor the brae, and
We twa' hae paid i't in the burn Frae

nev - er brought to mind? Should auld ac-quaint-ance
pu'd the Gow - ans fine. But we've wan - der'd mo -
morn - ing sun till dine; But seas be - tween us

be for - got, And days o' lang syne, For
ny a weary foot, Sin' Auld lang Syne. For
braid hae roar'd, Sin' Auld lang syne. For

© 2005 Sheet Music Digital

35

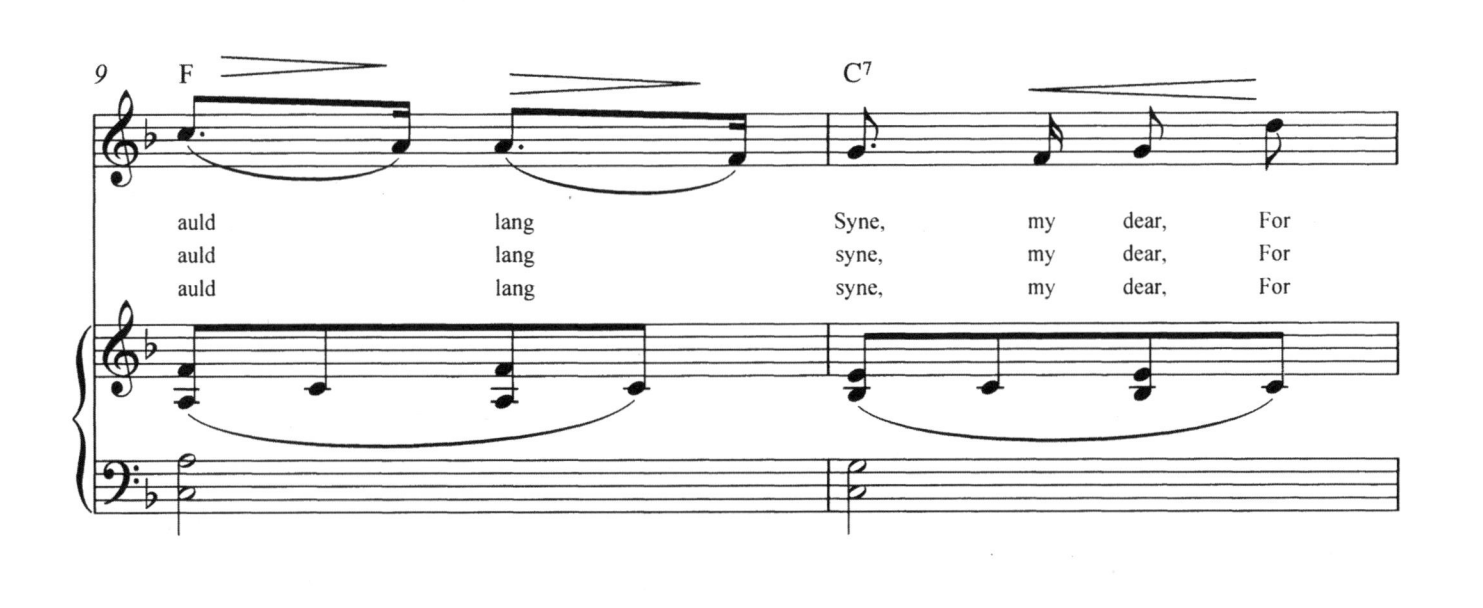

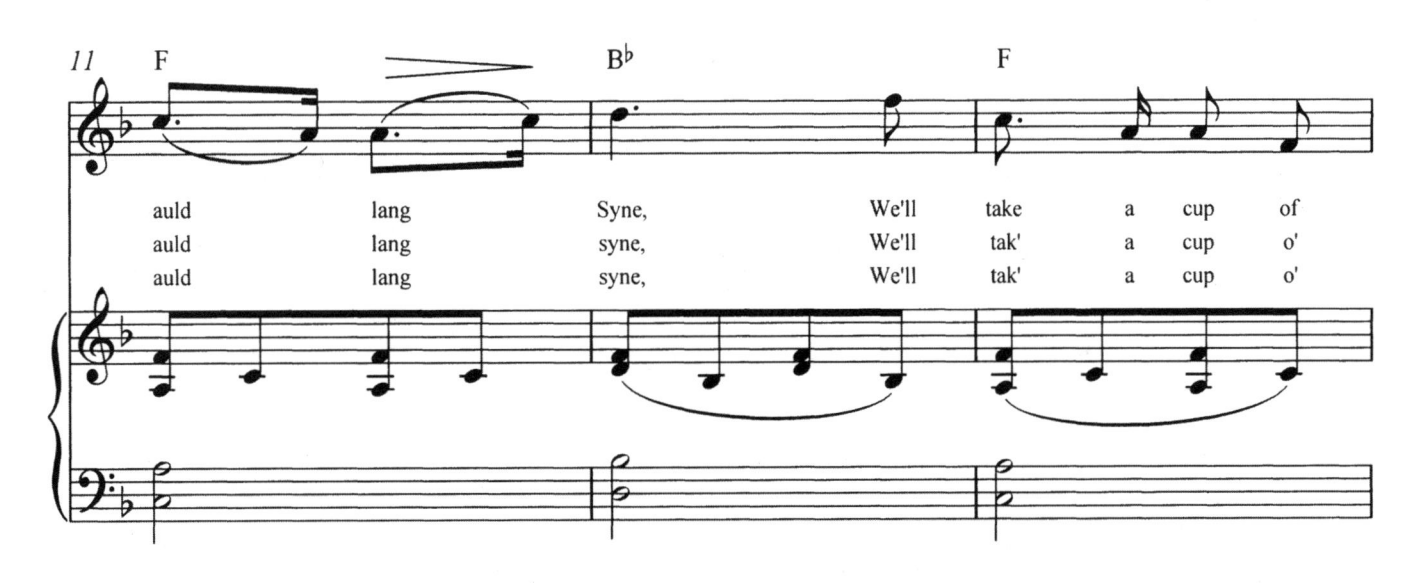

# The Blue Alsatian Mountains

Claribel (Charlotte Arlington Barnard)

STEPHEN ADAMS (1844-1913)
(PEN NAME OF MICHAEL MAYBRICK)

**Waltz tempo**

1. By the blue Alsatian mountains, Dwelt a maiden young and fair, _____ like the careless flowing fountains, Were the ripples of her hair, _____ Were the ripples of her hair; Angel mild her eyes so winning, Angel
2. By the blue Alsatian mountains, Dwelt a stranger in the spring, _____ And he linger'd by the fountains, Just to hear the maiden sing, _____ Just to hear the maiden sing; Just to whisper in the moonlight, Words the
3. By the blue Alsatian mountains, Many spring-times bloom'd and pass'd, _____ And the maiden in the fountains, Saw she lost her hopes at last, _____ She lost her hopes at last; And she wither'd like the flow-er That is

Public Domain

bright her hap - py smile, When be - neath the foun-tains spin - ning, You could hear her
sweet - est she had known, Just to charm a - way the hours Till her heart was
wait - ing for the rain, She will nev - er see the stran - ger, Where the foun - tains

song the while A - dé, A - dé, A - dé, Such songs will pass a - way
all his own A - dé, A - dé, A - dé, Such dreams may pass a - way
fall a - gain A - dé, A - dé, A - dé, The years have passed a - way

Tho' the blue Al - sa - tian moun - tains seem to watch and wait al - way.
But the blue Al - sa - tian moun - tains seem to watch and wait al - way.
But the blue Al - sa - tian moun - tains seem to watch and wait al - way.

# The Last Rose of Summer
## (Martha)

Sir John Stevenson (1761-1833)  Thomas Moore (1779-1833)

'Tis the last rose_ of_ sum-mer, Left bloom_ing a-lone; All her love-ly com-pan-ions Are_ fad_ed and gone. No_ flow-er of her

leave thee,_ thou_ lone one, To_ pine_ on the stem; Since the love-ly_ are sleep-ing, Go_ sleep_ thou with them; 'Thus kind-ly_ I

soon may_ I_ fol-low When_ friend-ships de-cay, And from love's shin-ing cir-cle The gems_ drop a-way! When true_ hearts lie

Public Domain

mf
kin - dred, No rose bud is nigh, To re - flect back her
scat - ter Thy leaves o'er the bed Where thy mates of the
wither - ed And fond ones are flown Oh! who would in -
1.-2.
3.
blush - es, Or give sigh for sigh. I'll not
gard - en Lie scent - less and dead. So
hab - it This bleak world a - lone? Oh!
who would in - hab - it This bleak world a-lone?
f

# The Loreley

Heinrich Heine (1823)

F. Silcher (1789-1860)
circ. 1837

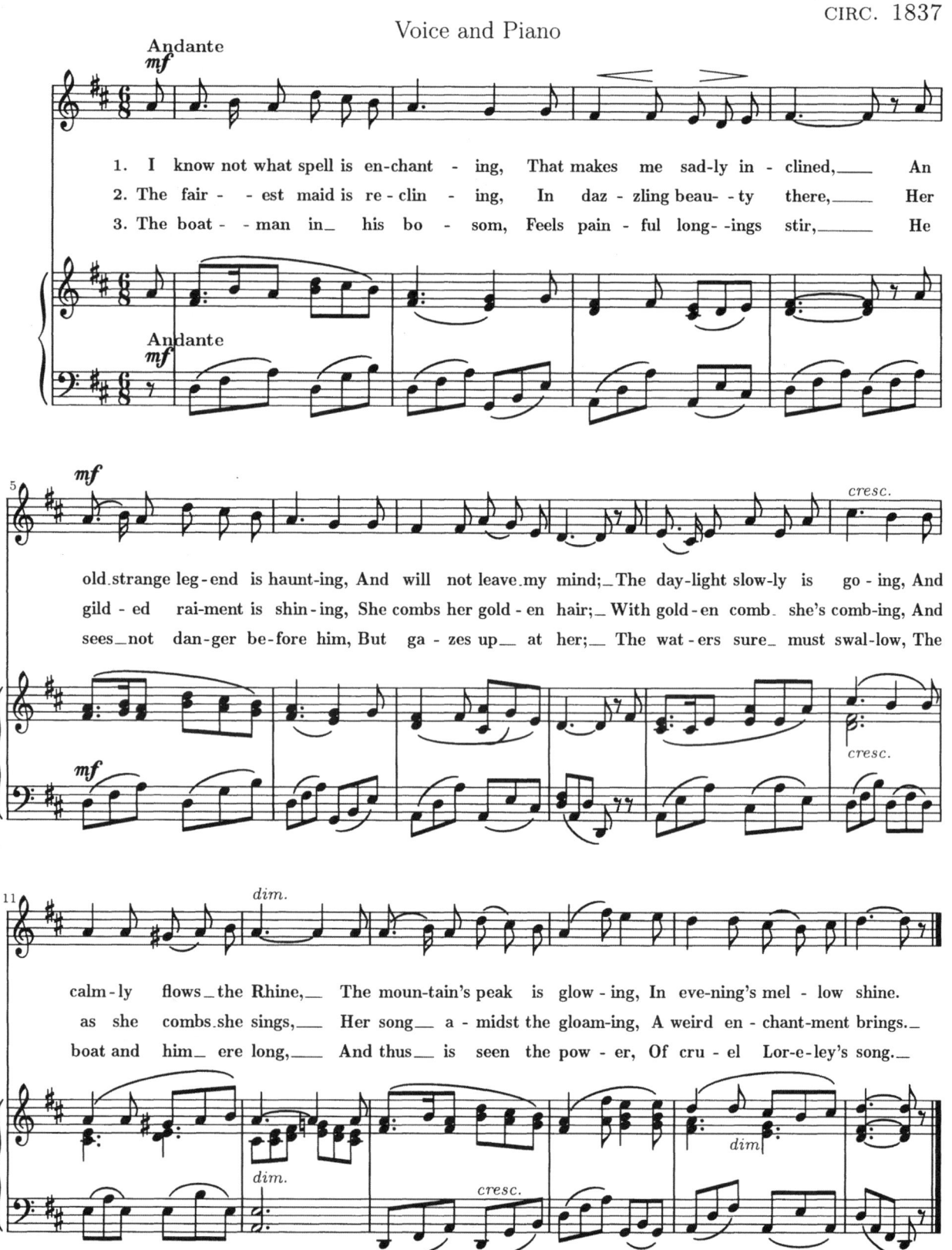

Voice and Piano

Andante

1. I know not what spell is en-chant - ing, That makes me sad-ly in - clined,____ An old strange leg-end is haunt-ing, And will not leave my mind;__ The day-light slow-ly is go - ing, And calm-ly flows__ the Rhine,__ The moun-tain's peak is glow - ing, In eve-ning's mel - low shine.
2. The fair - est maid is re - clin - ing, In daz - zling beau - ty there,____ Her gild - ed rai-ment is shin - ing, She combs her gold - en hair;__ With gold - en comb__ she's comb-ing, And as she combs she sings,__ Her song__ a - midst the gloam-ing, A weird en - chant-ment brings.__
3. The boat - man in__ his bo - som, Feels pain - ful long - ings stir,____ He sees__ not dan-ger be-fore him, But ga - zes up__ at her;__ The wat - ers sure__ must swal-low, The boat and him__ ere long,____ And thus__ is seen the pow - er, Of cru - el Lor-e-ley's song.__

# Oh, dear! what can the matter be?

*Traditional*

1. Oh, dear! what can the mat-ter be? Dear! dear! what can the mat-ter be? Oh, dear! what can the mat-ter be? John-ny's so long at the fair. He pro-mis'd he'd buy me a fair-ing should please me, And then for a kiss, oh, he vow'd he would tease me; He

2. Oh, dear! what can the mat-ter be? Dear! dear! what can the mat-ter be? Oh, dear! what can the mat-ter be? John-ny's so long at the fair. He pro-mis'd to buy me a bas-ket of po-sies, A gar-land of li-lies, a gar-land of ro-ses, A

pro-mis'd he'd bring me a bunch of blue rib-bons, To tie up my bon-ny brown hair.
lit-tle straw hat to set off the blue rib-bons That tie up my bon-ny brown hair.
And it's Oh, dear! what can the mat-ter be? Oh, dear! what can the mat-ter be? Oh, dear! what can the mat-ter be? John-ny's so long at the fair.

# Oh, Shenandoah

American Folk Song
arr, David Horace Davies

15
Shen-an - doah, I'm bound to leave you, A - way, you rol-ling riv - er, Oh,
15
19
Shen-an - doah, I'm bound to leave you, Look a - way, I'm bound a - way, a - cross the
19
23
wide Mis-sour - i. Look a - way, I'm bound a - way, a - cross the wide Mis-sour -
23

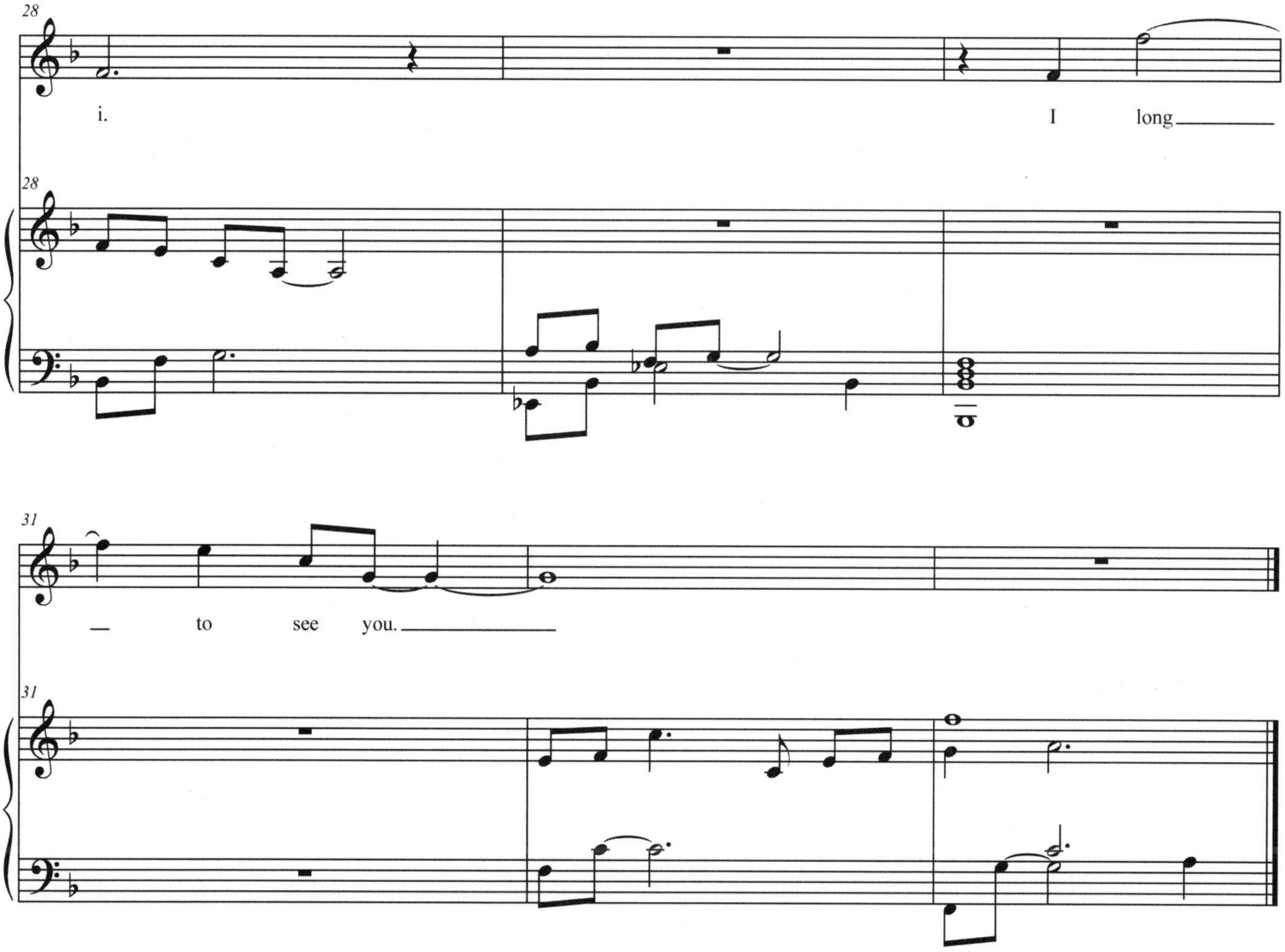
28
i.
I long
28
31
to see you.
31

# Sing Ivy

trad. (coll. G. B. Gardiner), arr. Gustav von Holst

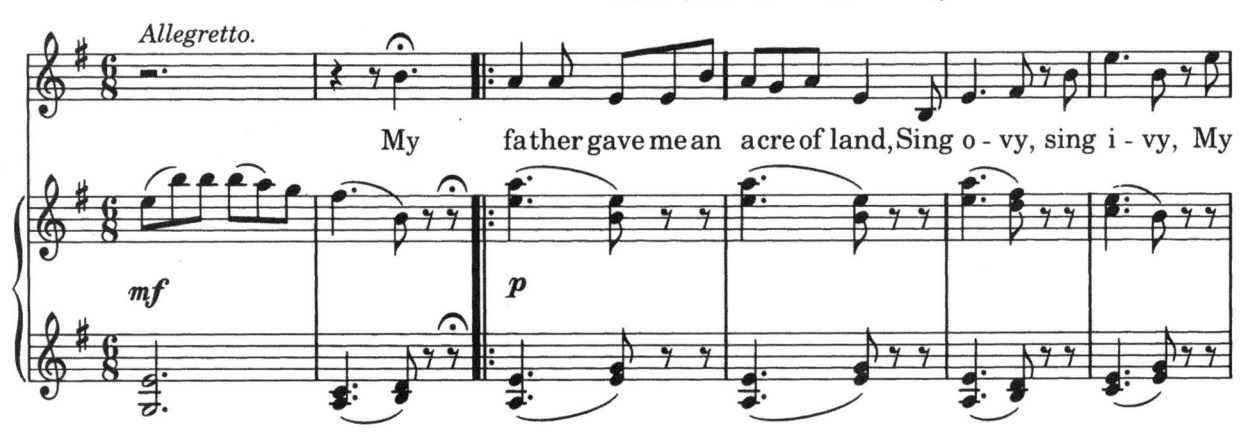

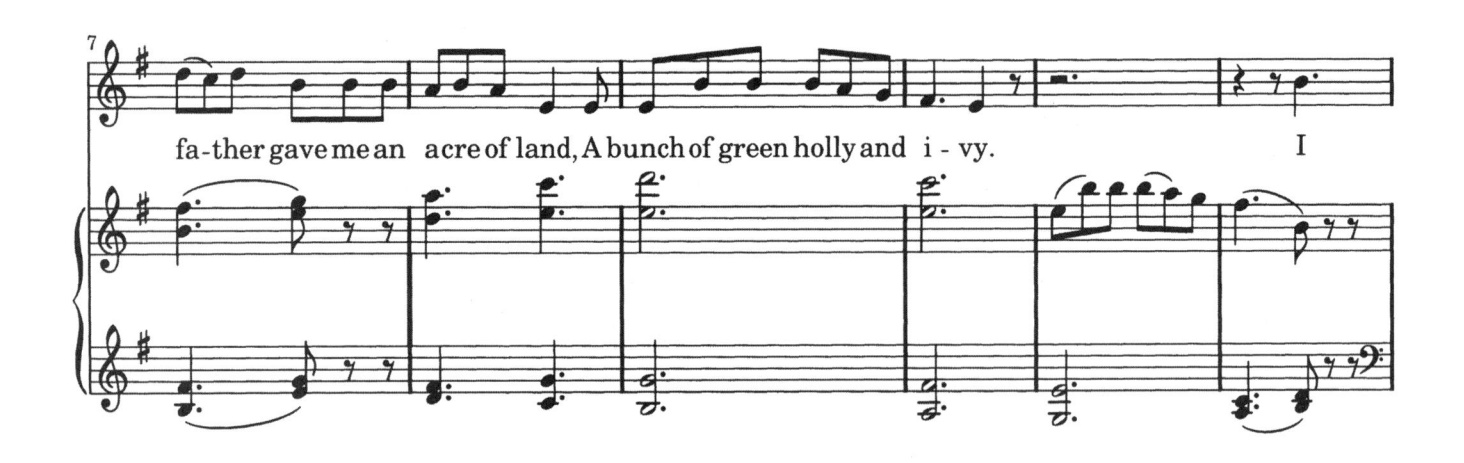

My father gave me an acre of land, Sing o-vy, sing i-vy, My father gave me an acre of land, A bunch of green holly and i-vy. I harrowed it with a bramble bush, Sing o-vy, sing i-vy, I harrowed it with a

Public Domain

1.-4.
5.
bramble bush, A bunch of green hol-ly and i - vy. I i - vy.
Poco animato.
cresc.
My team o' rats came rattling back, Sing o - vy, sing i - vy, My team o' rats came
cresc.
rattling back With fif ty bright guineas and an emp-ty sack, A bunch of green holly and i - vy.
cresc.
dim.
pp

## Additional Verses

**1.** My father gave me an acre of land,
   Sing ovy, sing ivy,
My father gave me an acre of land,
   A bunch of green holly and ivy.

**2.** I harrowed it with a bramble bush,
   Sing ovy, sing ivy,
I harrowed it with a bramble bush,
   A bunch of green holly and ivy.

**3.** I sowed it with two peppercorns,
   Sing ovy, sing ivy,
I sowed it with two peppercorns,
   A bunch of green holly and ivy.

**4.** I rolled it with a rolling-pin,
   Sing ovy, sing ivy,
I rolled it with a rolling-pin,
   A bunch of green holly and ivy.

**5.** I reaped it with my little penknife,
   Sing ovy, sing ivy,
I reaped it with my little penknife,
   A bunch of green holly and ivy.

**6.** I stowed it in a mouse's hole,
   Sing ovy, sing ivy,
I mowed it in a mouse's hole,
   A bunch of green holly and ivy.

**7.** I threshed it out with two beanstalks,
   Sing ovy, sing ivy,
I threshed it out with two beanstalks,
   A bunch of green holly and ivy.

**8.** I sent my rats to market with that,
   Sing ovy, sing ivy,
I sent my rats to market with that,
   A bunch of green holly and ivy.

**9.** My team o'rats came rattling back,
   Sing ovy, sing ivy,
My team o'rats came rattling back,
With fifty bright guineas and an empty sack
   A bunch of green holly and ivy.

---

Sheet music from www.MutopiaProject.org • *Free* to download, with the *freedom* to distribute, modify and perform.
Typeset using www.LilyPond.org by Nigel Holmes. Reference: Mutopia-2006/06/29-789
This sheet music has been placed in the public domain by the typesetter, for details see: http://creativecommons.org/licenses/publicdomain

# Slumber My Darling

Text by Stephen Collins Foster

STEPHEN COLLINS FOSTER
1826-1864

*Adagio*

Slum-ber, my dar-ling, thy moth-er is near, Guard-ing thy dreams from all ter-ror and fear,
Slumb-er, my dar-ling, till morn's blush-ing ray Brings to the world the glad tid-ings of day;

Sun-light has pass'd and the twi-light has gone, Slum-ber, my dar-ling, the night's com-ing on.
Fill the dark void with thy dream-y de-light— Slumb-er, thy moth-er will guard thee to-night,

Public Domain

17
Sweet vis-ions at-tend thy sleep, Fond-est, dear-est to me, While oth-ers their
Thy pil-low shall sa-cred be From all out-ward a-larms; Thou, thou are the
22
rev-els keep, I will watch o-ver thee. Slum-ber, my dar-ling, the birds are at rest, The
world to me In thine in-no-cent charms. Slum-ber, my dar-ling, the birds are at rest, The
27
wan-der-ing dews by the flow'rs are car-essed, Slum-ber, my dar-ling, I'll wrap thee up warm, And
wan-der-ing dews by the flow'rs are car-essed, Slum-ber, my dar-ling, I'll wrap thee up warm, And

pray that the an-gels will shield thee from harm.
pray that the an-gels will shield thee from harm.

# The Storm

Adelaide Procter
(1825-1864)

John Hullah
(1812-1884)

1. The tempest rages wild and high, The waves lift up their voice and cry Fierce answers to the angry sky
2. The thunders roar, the lightnings glare, Vain is it now to strive or dare; A cry goes up of great despair
3. Warm curtain'd was the little bed, Soft pillow'd was the little head, The storm will wake the child, they said

Public Domain

12
a piacere.
a tempo 1mo.
Mi-se-re-re Do - mi-ne. Thro' the black night and driv-ing rain, A ship is strug-gling,
Mi-se-re - re Do - mi-ne. The storm - y voi - ces of the main, The moan-ing wind and
Mi-se-re - re Do - mi-ne. Cow'ring a - mong his pil - lows white, He prays, his dim eyes
colla voce.
p
cres.
17
slentando.
a placere.
all in vain To live up - on the storm - y main.
pelt - ing rain, Beat on the nurs-'ry win-dow pane.
wild with fright, Fa - ther, save those at sea to-night! Mi-se-re - re Do-mi-ne, Mi-se-re - re
mf
sfz
colla voce.
23
un poco meno mosso.
Do - mi-ne.
4. The morn - ing shone, all clear and gay, On a
slentando
p

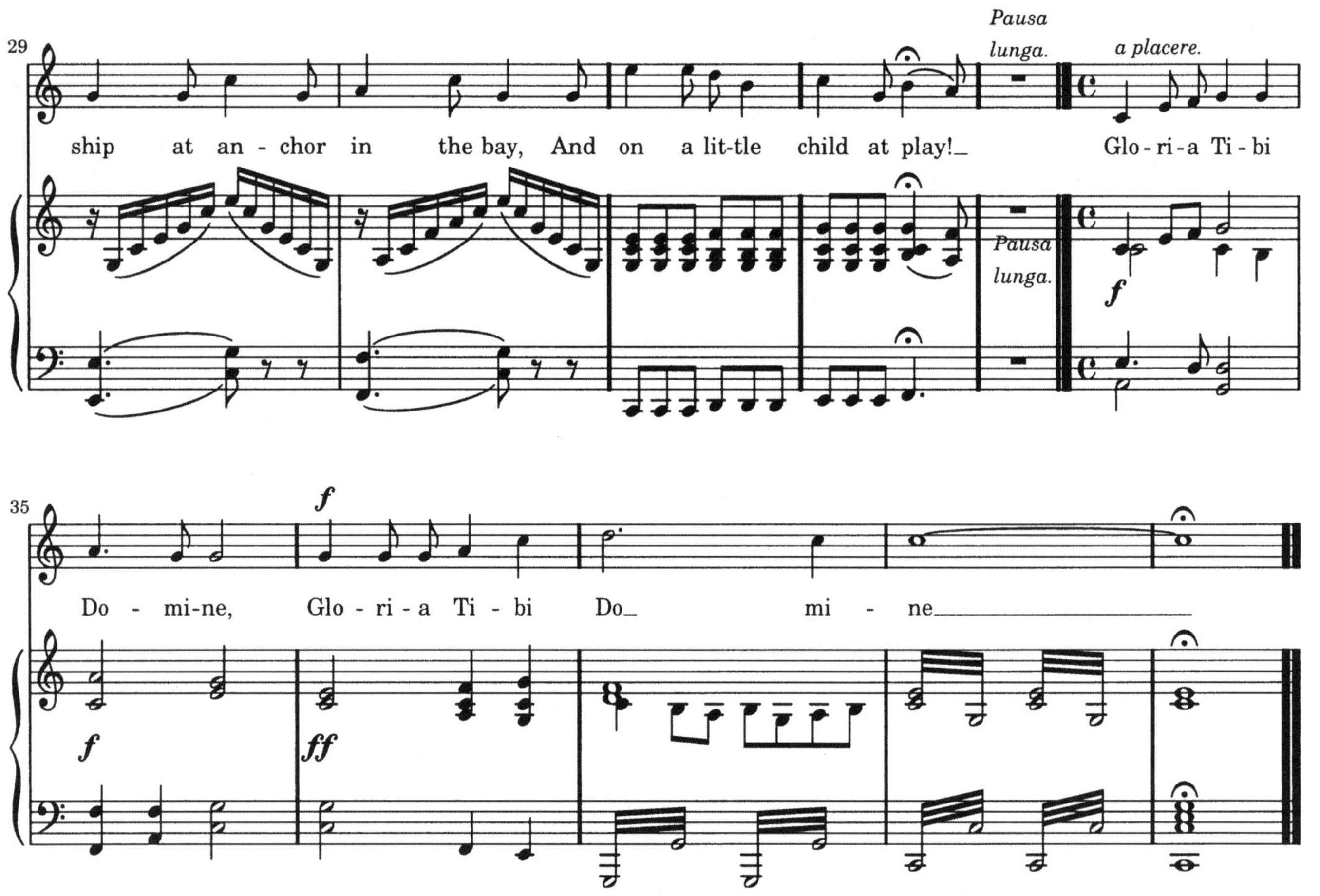

# There's Music in the Air

GEO. F. ROOT (1820-1895)

1. There's mu-sic in the air___ When the in-fant morn is nigh And faint its blush is seen___
2. There's mu-sic in the air___ When the noon-tide's sul-try beam Re-flects a gol-den light___
3. There's mu-sic in the air___ When the twi-light's gen-tle sigh Is lost on eve-ning's breast___

Public Domain

On the bright and laugh- ing sky.  Many a harp's ex - tat - ic sound
On the dis - tant mount- ain stream.  When be - neath some grate - ful shade
As its pen - sive beau - ties die.  Then, O then the loved ones gone

With it's thrill of joy pro-found  While we list en -chant-ed there  To the mu -sic in the
Sor-row's ach-ing head is laid  Sweet-ly to the spi - rit there Comes the mus -ic in the
Wake the pure ce - les-tial song  An - gel voi-ces greet us there  In the mu-sic of the

*2nd time* **pp**

air.
air.
air.

# AIN'T MISBEHAVIN'

Words by ANDY RAZAF
Music by THOMAS WALLER and HARRY BROOKS

Moderately

No-one to talk with, all by my-self, No one to walk with, but I'm hap-py on the shelf.

Ain't Mis-be-hav-in', I'm sav-in' my love for you.

I know for cer-tain the one I love I'm thru with flirt-in', it's just you I'm think-in' of,

Used With Permission

Eb Gb7 Fm7 Bb9 Eb Ab Bb7 G7 Cm
Ain't Mis-be-hav-in', I'm sav-in' my love for you. Like Jack Hor-ner
Ab7/C F7/C C7 Bb
in the cor-ner, don't go no-where, what do I care, Your kiss-es
Cm F7 Bb7 C7 F7 Bb7 Eb Cm7
are worth wait-in' for, be-lieve me I don't stay out late,
Fm7 Bb9 Eb G7+5 Ab Abm Ddim Eb Gb7
don't care to go I'm home a-bout eight, just me and my ra-di-o Ain't Mis-be-hav-in',
Fm7 Bb9 1 Eb C7 F7 Bb7 2 Eb Bb7 Eb
I'm sav-in' my love for you. you.
fz

# CRY ME A RIVER

Words and Music by
ARTHUR HAMILTON

Slowly and rhythmically

Now _____ you say you're lone-ly, _____ You cry the long night thru, _____ well, you can cry _____ me a riv-er, cry ___ me a riv-er, ___

Copyright © 1953, 1955 by Chappell & Co. and Momentum Music
Copyright Renewed
All Rights Administered by Chappell & Co.
International Copyright Secured   All Rights Reserved

Cm7
F7
Cm7/F
B♭6
B♭dim
E♭m6
Gm
E♭
I cried a riv - er o - ver
you.
Now
you say you're
Gm6
Gm7
Cm7
F13
F7♯5
B♭maj7
Am7
D7
sor - ry,
For be - in' so un - true,
well, you can
Dm7
Ddim
G7♯5
C9
Cm7
F7
Cm7/F
cry me a riv - er
cry me a riv - er,
I cried a riv - er o - ver

you. You drove me, near-ly drove me out of my head, While

**A la Bach (slightly faster)**

you nev-er shed a tear. Re-mem-ber? I re-mem-ber

all that you said; told me love was too ple - be-ian, Told me you were thru with me, an'

Gm Eb Gm6 Gm7 Cm7 F13 F7#5
Now you say you love me, Well just to prove you
Bbmaj7 Am7 D7 Dm7 Ddim G7#5 C9
do, Come on, an' cry me a riv - er, cry me a riv - er,
1. 2.
Cm7 F7 Cm7/F Bb6 D7#5(b9) Bb6
I cried a riv - er o - ver you. you.
Ped.

# DON'T GET AROUND MUCH ANYMORE

Words and Music by BOB RUSSELL
and DUKE ELLINGTON

Medium swing

When I'm not play-ing sol-i-taire, I take a book down from the shelf, and what with pro-grams on the air, I keep pret-ty much to my-

Used with Permission

© Copyright 1942 (Renewed 1970) Harrison Music Corp. and EMI Robbins Catalog Inc. in the U.S.A.
All Rights outside the U.S.A. Controlled by EMI Robbins Catalog Inc. (Publishing) and Warner Bros. Publications Inc. (Print)
International Copyright Secured   All Rights Reserved

G
no chord
C
Dm7
D♯dim7
C/E
self. Missed the Sat - ur - day dance,
heard they crowd-ed the
A7
Bm7
2fr
Cdim7
A7/C♯
D7
floor,
could - n't bear it with - out ___ you, _
G7
C6
don't get a - round much an - y more.
Thought I'd vis - it the
C
Dm7
D♯dim7
C/E
A7
Bm7
2fr
Cdim7
A7/C♯
club,
got as far as the door,

D7
they'd have asked me a - bout you,
G7
C6
C7
don't get a-round much an - y more.
F
Fm
Em7
C
Dar - ling I guess my mind's more at ease,
C7
F
F#m7♭5
4fr
B7
but, nev - er - the - less,

66

# MY FUNNY VALENTINE
(From "BABES IN ARMS")

Words by LORENZ HART
Music by RICHARD RODGERS

Slowly

My funny Valentine, Sweet comic Valentine,
You make me smile with my heart.
Your looks are laugh-a-ble, Un-pho-to-graph-a-ble,
Yet, you're my fav-'rite work of art. Is your

Used with Permission

fig- ure less than Greek; Is your mouth a lit- tle weak, when you
o- pen it to speak are you smart? But
don't change a hair for me, Not if you care for me,
Stay, lit- tle Val- en- tine, stay!
Each day is Val- en- tine's day.

*for Sharon*

# Ah, Holy Jesus

Johann Heermann, 1630
translated by Robert S. Bridges, 1899

"Herzliebster Jesu"
Johann Crüger, 1640
arranged by Richard Walters

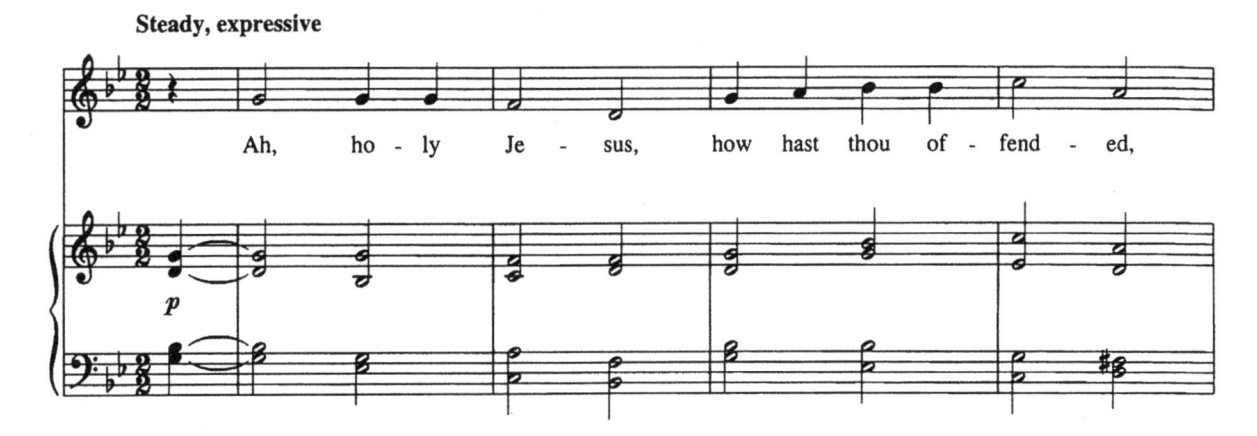

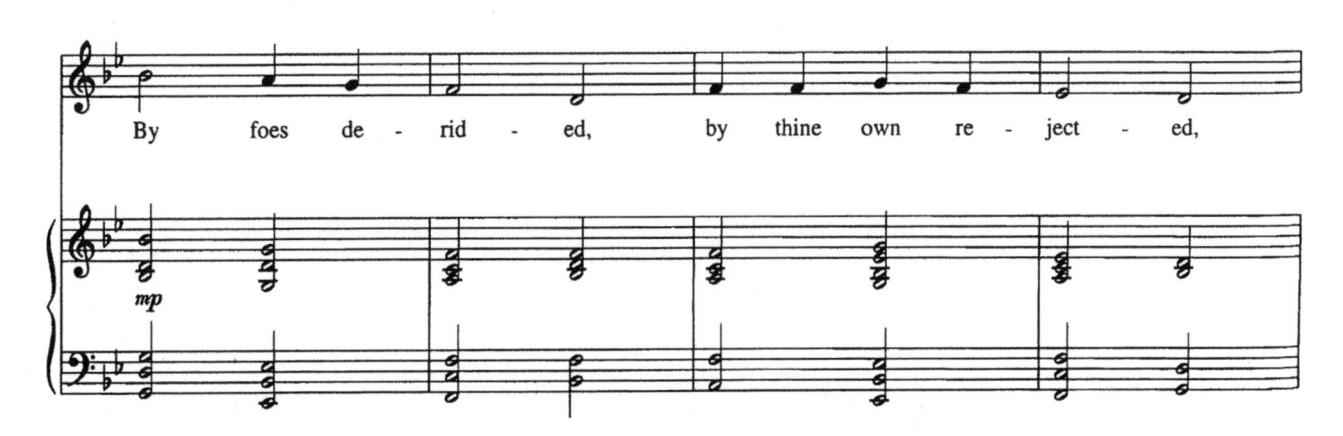

**Steady, expressive**

Ah, ho-ly Je-sus, how hast thou of-fend-ed,

That man to judge thee hath in hate pre-tend-ed?

By foes de-rid-ed, by thine own re-ject-ed,

Copyright © 1993 by HAL LEONARD CORPORATION
International Copyright Secured   All Rights Reserved

**Used with Permission**

O most afflicted! Who was the guilty? Who brought this upon thee? Alas, my treason, Jesus, hath undone thee! 'Twas I, Lord Jesus, I it was denied thee, I crucified thee.

For me, kind Jesus, was thy incarnation, Thy mortal sorrow, and thy life's oblation; Thy death of anguish and thy bitter passion, For my salvation.

**Slower**

Therefore, kind Jesus, Since I cannot pay Thee,

*mf warmly*

I do adore Thee, and will ever pray thee,

*cresc.* *f*

Think on thy pity and thy love unswerving,

*mf* *mp*

*molto rit.*

Not my deserving.

*p colla voce* *espressivo*

# I Wonder As I Wander

Traditional Appalachian Carol
**arr, David Horace Davies**

Lyrics: Je-sus the Sav-ior did come for to die for poor, orn-'ry peo-ple like you and like I; I won-der as I wan-der, out un-der the sky. When

Mary birthed Jesus, 'twas in a cow's stall, With wise men and farmers and shepherds and all. But high from God's heaven a star's light did fall, the prom-ise of

a - ges it\_ then did re - call. Hmm\_

## THE LORD IS MY SHEPHERD
### Unison voices with organ/piano

Psalm 23
R. L.

Music by
Robert Leaf

Lyrics beginning at m. 23: The Lord is my shep-herd, I shall not want, He

Copyright © 1980 Choristers Guild in the Choristers Guild LETTERS

Used with Permission

brings me to rest in the meadow land, Beside the still waters my soul is restored, He leads me in paths of righteousness.

Though I walk in the presence of death, I will fear no evil

55
pp
For His rod and His staff, they com - fort me, They
60
com - fort me.
pp
mp
65
70
p
Though
p
75
foes are a - round me, He sets my feast, My head is a - noint-ed, my

cup o'er-flows, For-ev-er I'll dwell in the house of the Lord, For He is my shep-herd, I shall not want.

105
The Lord is my shep-herd, I shall not want, He brings me to
110
115
rest in the mea - dow land, Be - side the still wa-ters my soul is re -
120
stored. The Lord is my shep-herd, I shall not want.
125
molto rit.
pp

# O HOLY NIGHT
(Cantique de Noël)

By ADOLPHE ADAM

Andante maestoso

O ho - ly night! The stars are bright - ly shin - ing, It is the night of our dear Sav - iour's birth; Long lay the world in sin and er - ror

Mi - nuit, Chré - tien, c'est l'heu - re so - len - nel - le Où l'Hom - me Dieu des - cen - dit jus - qu'a nous, Pour ef - fa - cer la ta - che o - ri - gi -

pin - - - ing, Till he ap-pear'd, and the soul felt its
nel - - le Et de son père ar - rê - ter le cour-

worth. A thrill of hope the
roux. Le mon - de en - tier tres -

*cresc.*

wear - y world re-joic - es, For yon - der breaks a
sail - le d'es - pé - ran - ce A cet - te nuit qui

new and glo - rious morn. Fall on your
lui donne un sau - veur. Peu - - ple, à ge -

knees! Oh hear the an-gel voi-ces! O night di-vine! O night when Christ was born, O night di-

noux! At-tends ta dé-li-vran-ce. No-ël! No-ël! voi-ci le Ré-demp-teur, No-

*cresc.*

vine! O night, O night di-
ël! voi - ci le Ré - demp-

vine.
teur.

Led by the
De no - tre

light of Faith se-rene-ly beam - ing, With glow-ing
foi que la lu-mière ar-den - te nous gui - de

hearts by his cra - dle we stand;
tous au ber- ceau de l'en- fant,

So, led by light of a star sweet - ly gleam - ing, Here came the wise men from the O - rient land.
comme au - tre - fois une é - toi - le bril - lan - te y con - dui - sit les chefs de l'o - ri - ent.

The King of Kings lay
Le Roi des Rois naît

thus in lowly manger, In all our trials is
dans une humble crèche; puissants du jour, fiers

born to be our friend; He knows our
de votre grandeur, à votre or-

need, to our weakness no
gueil c'est de là qu'un Dieu

stranger; Behold your
prêche; courbez vos

King! be- fore the low- ly
fronts de- vant le Ré- demp-

bend! Be- hold your
teur, cour- bez vos

*cresc.*

King! your King! be- fore Him
fronts de- vant le Ré- demp-

*dim.*

bend!
teur.

mf
Tru - ly He
Le Ré - demp-
tr
mf
taught us to love one an - oth - er; His law is
teur a bri - sé toute en - tra - ve, La terre est
love and His Gos - pel is Peace.
li - bre et le ciel est ou - vert.
Chains shall He break, for the slave is our
Il voit un frè - re où né - tait qu'un es -

broth - er, And in His name all op-pres-sion shall
cla - ve, L'a-mour u-nit ceux qu'en-chaî-nait le

cease. Sweet hymns of joy in
fer. Qui lui di-ra no-

grate-ful cho-rus raise we, Let all with-in us
tre re-con-nais-san - ce? C'est pour nous tous qu'il

praise His Ho-ly name. Fall on your
naît, qu'il souf-fre et meurt. Peu - ple, dé-

knees! Oh hear the an - gel
bout, chan - - te ta dé - li -
voic - es! O night di -
vran - ce, No - ël! No -
vine! O night when Christ was
ël! chan - tons le Ré - demp-
born, O night di -
teur, No - ël! No -
cresc.
cresc.

vine! O night, O night di -
ël! chan - tons le Ré - demp -
vine!
teur.
dim. e rit.

# Pie Jesu
## from
## REQUIEM

Gabriel Fauré

9
un poco più
Pi - e Je - su
p
12
mf
Do - mi - ne, do - na e - is re - qui - em,
meno p
mf
15
p
do - na e - is re - qui - em.
dim.
p

17
dolce
Do -
19
na, ___ do - na, Do - mi - ne, do - na e - is
22
poco cresc.
re - qui - em, sem - pi - ter - nam re - qui - em,

sem - pi - ter - nam re - qui - em,

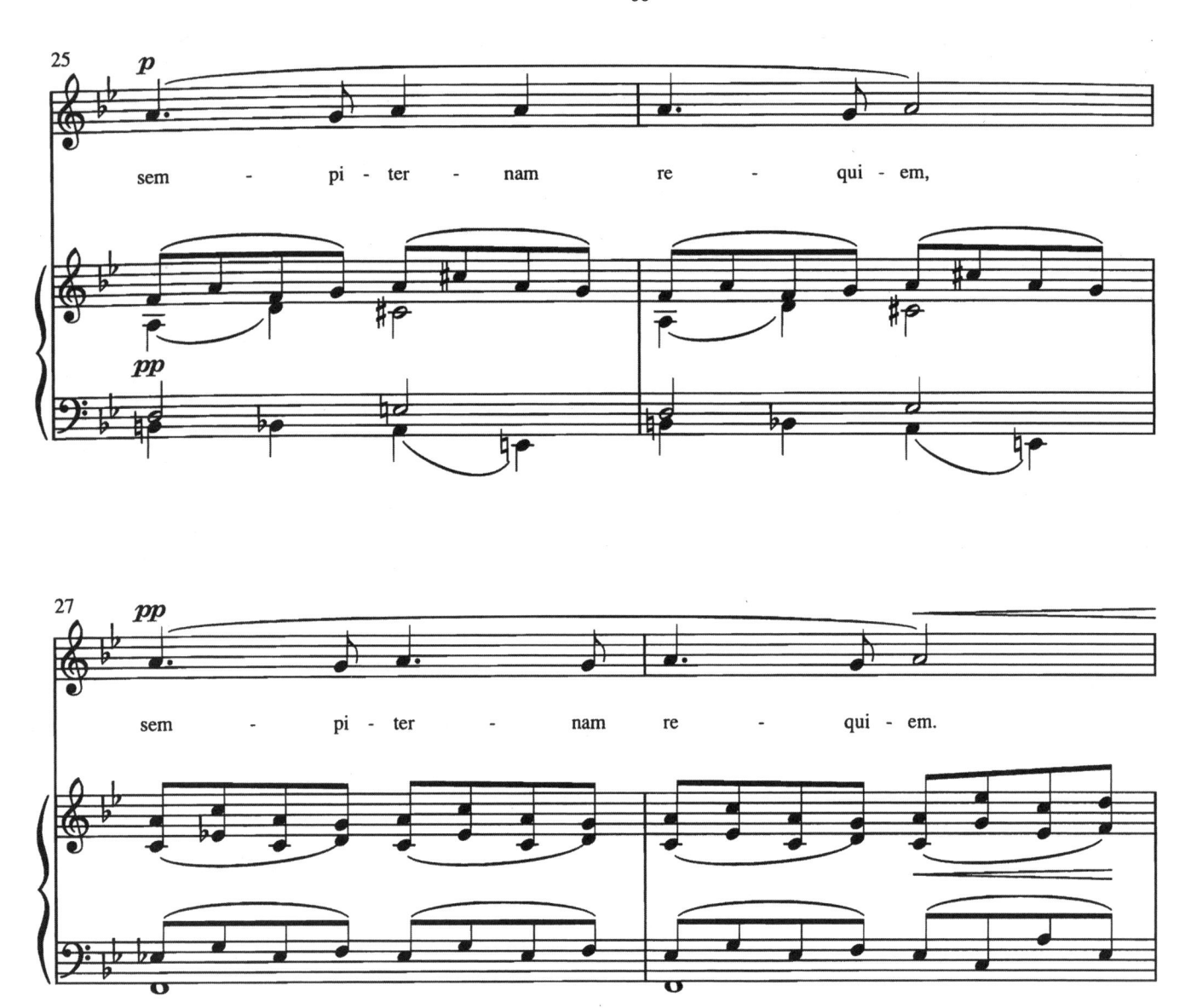

sem - pi - ter - nam re - qui - em.

Pi - e, pi - e Je - su, pi - e - Je - su,

32
Do - mi - ne do - na e - is do - na e - is
35
sem - pi ter - nam re - qui - em,
pp
37
poco ritenuto
sem - pi - ter - nam re - qui - em.
poco ritenuto

# Simple Gifts

Shaker Song (18th Century)
arr, David Horace Davies

'Tis the gift to be sim-ple, 'tis the gift to be free, 'tis the gift to come down where we ought to be, and when we find our-selves in the place just right, 'twill be in the val-ley of love and de-light.

Faster (♩ = c. 104)
14
'Tis the gift to be sim-ple, 'tis the gift to be free, 'tis the
Pno.
18
gift to come down where we ought to be, and when we find our-selves in the place just right, 'twill
22
be in the val-ley of love and de-light. When true sim - plic-t - ty is gained to bow and to bend we
27
shan't be a-shamed, to turn, turn, will be our de-light 'till by turn - ing, turn - ing we

come 'round right.

When true sim-plic-i-ty is gained to bow and to bend we shan't be a-shamed, to turn, turn, will be our de-light, 'till by turn-ing, turn-ing we come 'round right. 'Tis a gift to be sim-ple, 'tis a gift to be free!

# Befiehl dem Herrn deine Wege!

Max Reger, 1902
Commit thy way unto the Lord; trust also in him, and he shall bring it to pass
Psalm 37:5

11
mp
crescendo
fe auf ihn, er wird's wohl
mp
crescendo
Be - fiehl dem Hern
11
16
p
p
ma - - - chen, und hof - fe, hof - fe auf ihn. Be -
p
dei - ne We - - - - - ge und hof - fe auf ihn.
16

21
f
f
fiehl, be - fiehl dem Hern dei - ne We - ge und hof
p
f
Be - fiehl dem Hern dei - ne We - ge
21
26
p
e sempre crescendo
fe und hof - fe auf ihn, be - fiehl dem Hern dei - ne
p
e sempre crescendo
be - fiehl dem Hern dei - ne
26

30
ff
We - ge und hof - - - - - - - - - - - fe und
ff
We - ge und hof - fe, und hof - - - - - - fe, und
30
ff
34
p
f
hof - fe auf ihn,
Be - fiehl dem
p
f
hof - fe auf ihn.
Be -
34
p

38
Hern dei - ne We - - - - ge und
fiehl dem Harn dei - - - ne We - ge und
38
41
rit.
p
hof - fe und hof - fe auf ihn.
rit.
p
hof - fe, und hof - fe auf ihn.
41
p

45
p
Be -
p
Be - fiehl dem
45
p
ppp sempre ben legato
senza Ped.
50
fiehl dem Hern dei - ne We - ge und hof - fe auf
Hern dei - ne We - ge und hof - fe, und hof - fe auf
50

Note:

This also can be done wth Soprano alone, with the organ or harmonium accompaniment.

# Commit Thy Ways to the Lord

Max Reger, 1902
Edited and translated by Paul Stetsenko
Psalm 37:5

11
mp
crescendo
on Him, He will de - - -
mp
crescendo
Com - mit thy ways
11
16
li - - - ver, re - ly re - ly on Him Com
p
p
to the Lord God, re ly on Him.
p
16

mit com - mit thy ways to the Lord God, re ly,
Com - mit thy ways to the Lord God,
re ly on Him, com - mit thy ways to the
e sempre crescendo
e sempre crescendo
com - mit thy ways to the

ff
30
Lord God, re ly, re
ff
Lord God, re ly re - ly, re
30
ff
34
p
f
ly on Him, Com - mit thy
p
f
ly on Him, Com -
34
p

ways to the Lord God, re-
mit thy ways to the Lord God, re-
ly, re ly on Him
ly, re ly on Him.

*senza Ped.*

46
p
Com - mit thy
p
Com - mit thy ways to the
46
p
ppp sempre ben legato
51
ways to the Lord God, re - ly on Him,
Lord God, re - ly on, re - ly on Him, then
51
ppp

Note:

This also can be done wth Soprano alone, with the organ or harmonium accompaniment.

# Jesus Lover of My Soul

David Horace Davies

117

32
right - eous - ness. Ooo
mp
Thou art full of truth and grace.
f
False and full of sin I am. Ooo
f
mp
37
f Plent - eous grace with Thee is found, grace to cov - er all my sin,
Ooo
mp
f Plent - eous grace with Thee is found grace to cov - er all my sin
f Plent - eous grace with Thee is found, grace to cov - er all my sin,
42
let the heal - ing streams a - bound, make and keep me pure with - in. Thou of life the
let the heal - ing streams a - bound, make and keep me pure with - in. Thou of life the
let the heal - ing streams a - bound, make and keep me pure with - in. Thou of life the

119

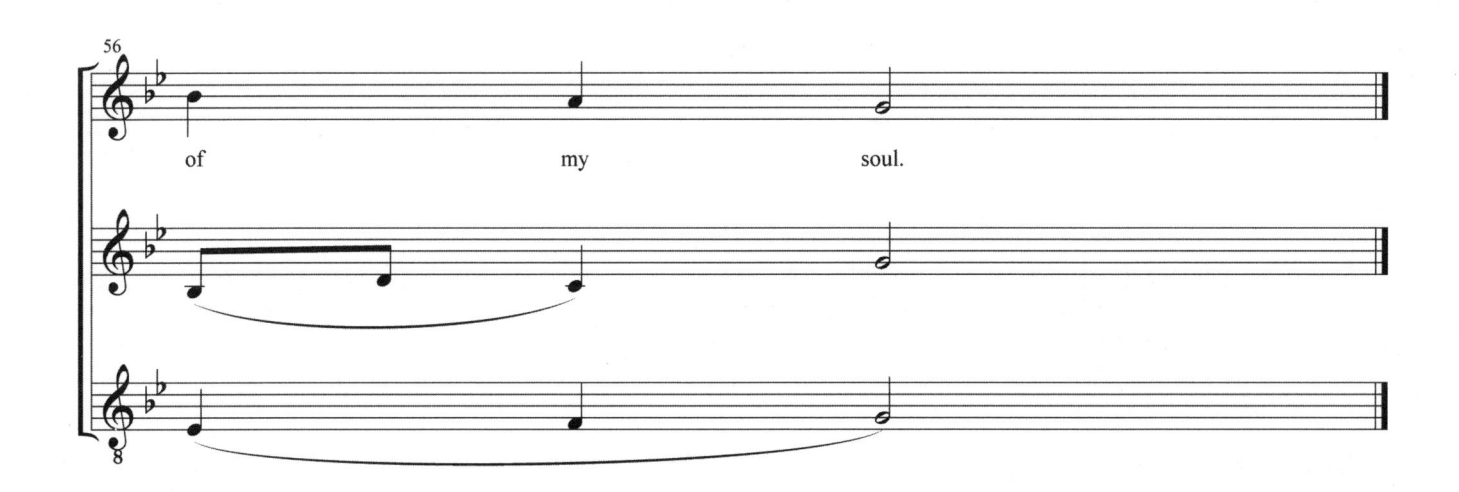

# Laudate Dominum

ad una o die voci pari

Lorenzo Perosi

18
Do - mi-ni ma-net in ae - ter - - num. Glo - ri - a Pa - tri,
18
24
et Fi - li - o, et Spi - ri - tu - i San - - - cto.
24
30
Si - cut e - rat in prin - ci - pi - o, et nunc, et sem - per,
30

et in sae-cu - la sae-cu-lo-rum. A - men, a - men.

# Magnificat

Lento

Peter Benoit (1834-1901)

Magni-fi-cat a-nima mea dominum, et exsultavit spi-ritus me-us in de-o sa-lu-ta-ri me - o.

Magni-fi-cat a-nima mea dominum, et exsultavit spi-ritus me-us in de-o sa-lu-ta-ri me - o.

Magni-fi-cat a-nima mea dominum, et exsultavit spi-ritus me-us in de-o sa-lu-ta-ri me - o.

Organ — Grand Jeu.

Quia res-pe-xit humili-ta-tem ancillae su - ae, ec-ce enim ex hoc be-atam me di-cent omnes gene-ra-ti-o-nes,

Qui-a fe-cit mihi mag-na qui potens est, et sanctum nomen e - ius, et miseri-cor-dia e - ius

Qui-a fe-cit mihi mag-na qui potens est, et sanctum nomen e - ius,

Qui-a fe-cit mihi mag-na qui potens est, et sanctum nomen e - ius,

Creative Commons Attribution-ShareAlike 3.0

39
a pro-ge - ni-e in pro-ge - nies timentibus e - um. Fe-cit po-ten-tiam in brachio su-o, dis persit super-
Fe-cit po-ten-tiam in brachio su-o, dis persit super-
Fe-cit po-ten-tiam in brachio su-o, dis persit super-
Grand Jeu
51
bos mente cordis su - i, de - po-suit po-tentes de se-de et exal - ta - vit hu - mi - les
bos mente cordis su - i, de - po-suit po-tentes de se-de et exal - ta - vit hu - mi - les
bos mente cordis su - i, de - po-suit po-tentes de se-de et exal - ta - vit hu - mi - les e-su-ri - en-tes implevit bo - nis,
p
pp
64
et di - vi-tes dimisit in - a - nes, suscepit Is-ra-el pu-erum su - um. Re-cor - da-tus mise-ri - cor-diae
tr

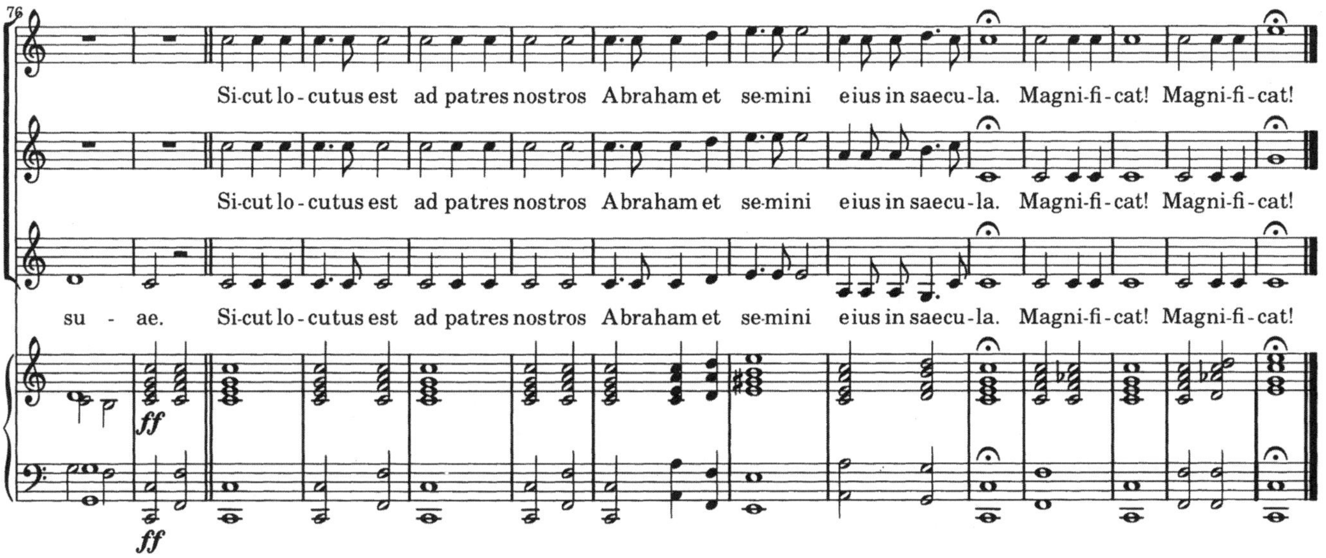

# Out of Your Sleep Arise and Wake

circa 14-15th century
R. Mather 1996

Brightly

1. Out of your sleep a-rise and wake!
2. And through a maid-en fair and wise.
3. Now man is bright-er than the sun:
4. Now, bless-ed broth-er grant us grace,

1. rise and wake;
2. fair and wise;
3. that the sun;
4. grant us grace;

9
S 1
For God man - kind now hath y - take All of a
Now man is made of full great price; Now an-gels
Now man in heav'n on high shall won; Bless - ed be
at doom - es day to see thy face, And in thy
S 2
hath y - take All of a
full great price. Now an-gels
high shall won. Bless - ed be
see thy face. And in thy
9
Pno.
13
S 1
maid with - out a - ny make. Of all wo - men she bear - eth
knee - len to man's ser - vyse, And at this time all this
God this game is be - gun. And his moth - er that bear - eth
court to have a place, That we may there sing thee
S 2
maid with - out a - ny make. Bear - - - eth
knee - len to man's ser - vyse, all this
God this game is be - gun bear - - - eth
court to have a place, sing thee
13
Pno.

the bell. / be-fell. / the bell. / no-well.

Glo-ry to God. Glo-ry to God. Glo-ry to God. Glo-ry to God. Glo-ry to God in the high-est.

the bell. / be-fell. / the bell. / no-well.

Glo-ry to God. Glo-ry to God. Glo-ry to God. Glo-ry to God. Glo-ry to God in the high-est.

25
Glo - ry to God. Glo - ry to God. Glo - ry to God in the high - est.
Glo - ry to God. Glo - ry to God. Glo - ry to God in the high - est.
25

# Puer Natus in Bethlehem

Josef Rheinberger
op. 118 no. 6

11
ja - cet in prae - se - pi - o qui reg - nat si - ne ter - mi -
o qui re - nat si - ne ter - mi -
11
16
no. Re - ges de Sa - ba ve - ni - unt
no. Re - ges de Sa - ba ve - ni - unt
16
f
Man.

au - rem thus myr - rham of - fe - runt Si - ne ser -
pen - tis vul - ne - re, de nos - tro ve -
pen - tis vul - ne - re, de nos - tro ve - nit

31
mf
nit san - gui - ne, in - car - ne no - bis
mf
san - gui ne, in car - ne no - bis si - mi -
31
36
ff
so - mi - lis, pec - ca - to sed dis - si - mi - lis ut
ff
lis, pec - ca - to sed dis - si - mi - lis ut
36
f

red- der et nos ho- mi- nes, De- o et
red- der et nos ho- mi- nes, De- o et

si- bi si- mi- les. In
si- bi si- mi- les. In

hoc na - ta - li gau - di - o, in hoc na -
hoc na - ta - li gau - di - o, in hoc na -
ta - li gau - di - o: be - ne - di - ca - mus
ta - li gau - di - o: be - ne - di - ca - mus

136

71
de - tur sanc - ta tr - ni - tas, lau - de - tur
de - tur sanc - ta tri - ni - tas, lau - de - tur
71
76
sanc - ta tri - - - - - ni - tas, De - o di -
sanc - ta tri - - - - - ni - tas, De - o dic -
76

ca - mus gra - ti - as, De - o di - ca - mus

ca - mus gra - ti - as, De - o di - ca - mus

gra - ti - as.

gra - ti - as.

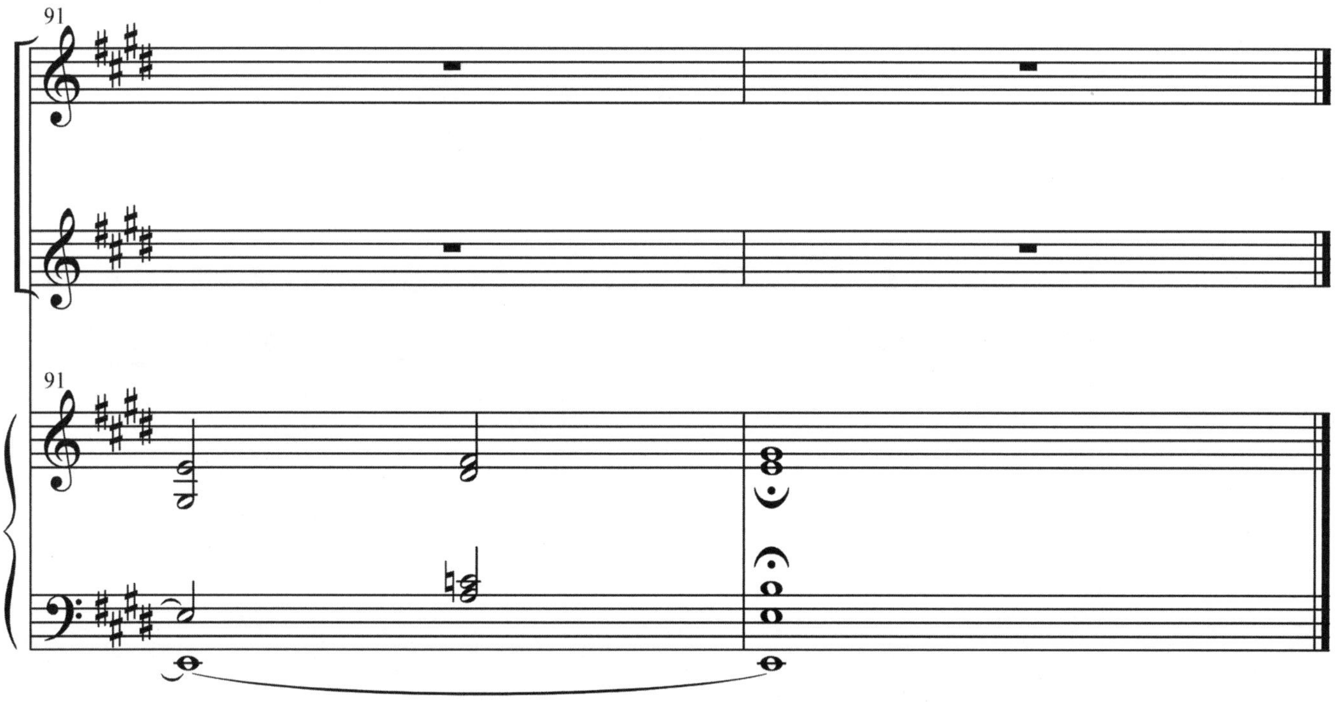
91
91

# An die Musik

FRANZ SCHUBERT
Op.88. No 4.

Moderato

Du hol - de Kunst, in wie viel grau - en Stun - den, wo mich des Le - bens wil - der Kreis um - strickt, hast du mein Herz zu

Oft hat ein Seuf - zer, dei - ner Harf' ent - floss - en ein su - sser hei - li - ger Ac - cord von dir, den Him - mel bess' - rer warmer Lieb' entzunden, hast mich in eine bess're Welt entrückt, in eine bess're Welt entrückt.

Zeiten mir erschlossen, du holde Kunst, ich danke dir dafür, du holde Kunst, ich danke dir.

# An die Musik

FRANZ SCHUBERT
Op.88. No 4.

war-mer Lieb' ent - zun - den, hast mich in ei - ne bess' - re Welt ent-
Zei - ten mir er - schlos-sen, du hol - de Kunst, ich dan - ke dir da-

rückt, in ei - ne bess' - re Welt ent-rückt.
fur, du hol - de Kunst, ich dan - ke dir.

# FINDING HOME

Lyric by TINA LANDAU
Music by RICKY IAN GORDON

Simple, Slow (♩ = 60)

Molto legato

SARAH:
Find-ing home in an un-ex-pect-ed way. Mak-ing a home day by day. Be-ing

Used with Permission

home in an un-en-cum-bered sleep. Stay-ing at home sweet and deep. Leav-ing home un-ex-pect-ed-ly and then: Search-ing for home once a-gain. If you keep it in your heart

*pp*

when you are forced to roam  I know you too will start finding home. Finding home in an un-fa-mi-liar face; feel-ing your home, find-ing grace. Keep-ing

*Freely* ... *rit.* ... **A tempo**

147

*home in the gestures that you know; holding home if you go. Trusting home if you travel far and wide. Carrying home deep inside. Deep inside.*

# Charles B. Griffin

## *Three Emily Dickinson Songs*

for soprano and piano
ca. 8'

### Charles B. Griffin
82-67 Austin Street #710
Kew Gardens, NY 11415
(718)850-8927
charlesbgriffin@earthlink.net
www.charlesgriffin.net

The poetry of Emily Dickinson is reprinted with permission of the publishers and
the Trustees of Amherst College from The Poems of Emily Dickinson ,
edited by Thomas H. Johnson, Cambridge, MA: The Belknap Press of Harvard University Press,
Copyright 1951, 1955, 1979, 1983 by the President and Fellows of Harvard College.

Music © 1991 Charles B. Griffin / Coriolis Press - ASCAP
All Rights Reserved

Used with permission

# Heart! We will forget him!

**Emily Dickinson**

Soprano Solo with Piano

**Charles B. Griffin**

11
f
mf
warmth he gave I will for - get the light! When you have done, pray
f
mf
15
ff
mf
tell me That I my thoughts may dim!
ff
mf
18
mp
rit
slowly
p
Haste! lest while you're lag - ging I may re - mem - ber
rit
slowly
mp
p

him!

**Emily Dickinson**

# I felt a Funeral

Soprano Solo with Piano

**Charles B. Griffin**

Waltz-like
♩ = ca. 110-120

21
sense was break - ing — through
And when they all — were seat - ed, —
28
A Ser - vice, — like a Drum
Kept beat - ing — beat - ing —
35
till I thought My Mind was go - ing numb
f
Piu mosso
Piu mosso
f

41
(sim.)
47
poco rit.
A Tempo
mp
And then I heard them lift a Box And creak a - cross my Soul With those same
poco rit.
A Tempo
mp
51
ff
Piu mosso
(as before)
Boots of Lead, a - gain, Then Space be - gan to toll,
Piu mosso
(as before)
ff
mf

Meno mosso
Molto Rubato
p dolce
As all the Heav - ens were a
poco a poco rit.
rall. molto
Meno mosso
Molto Rubato
p
Bell, And Be - ing, but an Ear, And I, and Sil - ence, some strange Race Wrecked,
poco a poco accel.
poco a poco accel.
Tempo Primo
mp
sol - i - tar - y, here And then a Plank in Rea - son broke, And
Tempo Primo
mp

74
I dropped down, and down
77
And hit a World, at ev - ery plunge, and Fin - ished know - ing
82
then
poco rit.

# Because I could not stop for Death

**Emily Dickinson**

Soprano Solo with Piano

**Charles B. Griffin**

Allegro agitato ♩·=ca. 120

© 1991 Charles B. Griffin

9
sf mp
11
mf
Be - cause I
13
could not stop for Death He kind - ly stopped for

159

slow - ly drove____ He knew no haste____

____ And I had put a - way____ My la - bor and____ my

lei - sure too,____ For His Ci - vil - i - ty____ We

passed the School, where Chil-dren strove At Re-cess in the Ring We passsed the fields of Ga-zing Grain We passed the Set-ting Sun Or ra-ther He passed Us The

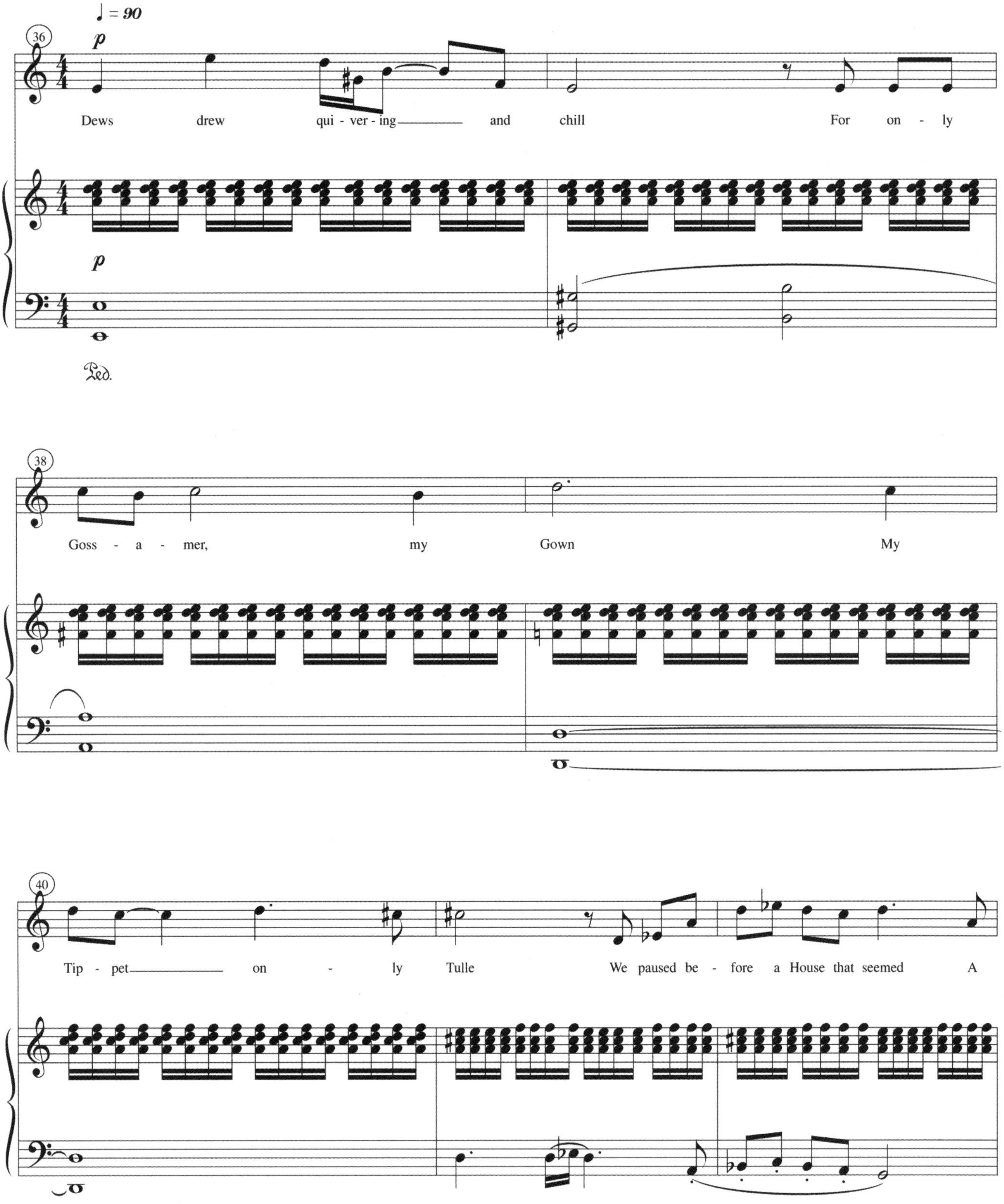
♩ = 90
36
p
Dews drew qui - ver - ing and chill For on - ly
p
Ped.
38
Goss - a - mer, my Gown My
40
Tip - pet on - ly Tulle We paused be - fore a House that seemed A

Swel-ling of the Ground  The Roof was scarce-ly vis - i-ble  The Cor-nice in the Ground  Since then  'tis Cen - tu - ries and yet  Feels short - er than the Day  I first surmised the Hor- ses' Heads_____ Were toward E - ter - ni -

**Tempo Primo**

ty_____

*accel. poco a poco*

# Waiting
*for low voice & piano*

Words & Music by
**WILLIAM CAMPBELL**

Slow & Comfortable (♩ = ca. 64)

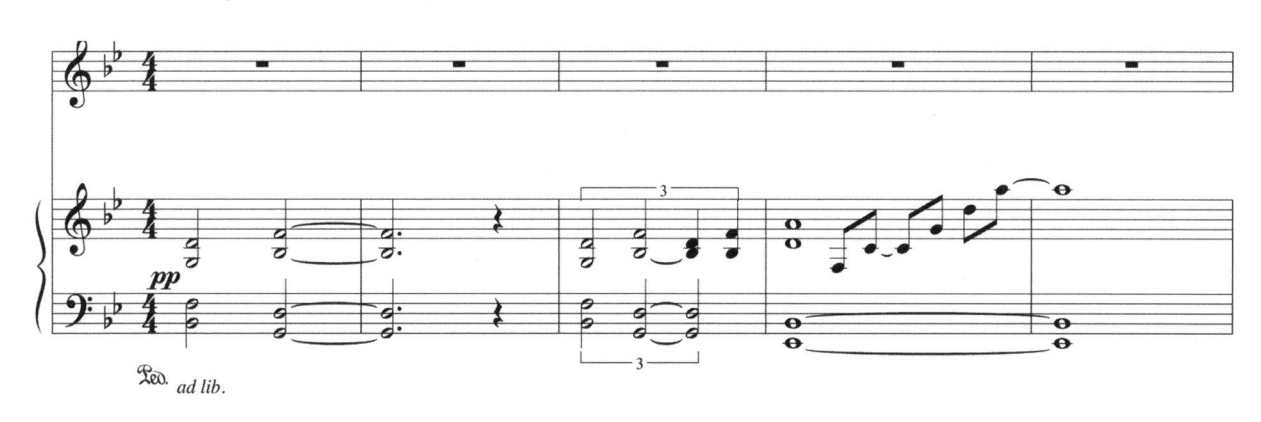

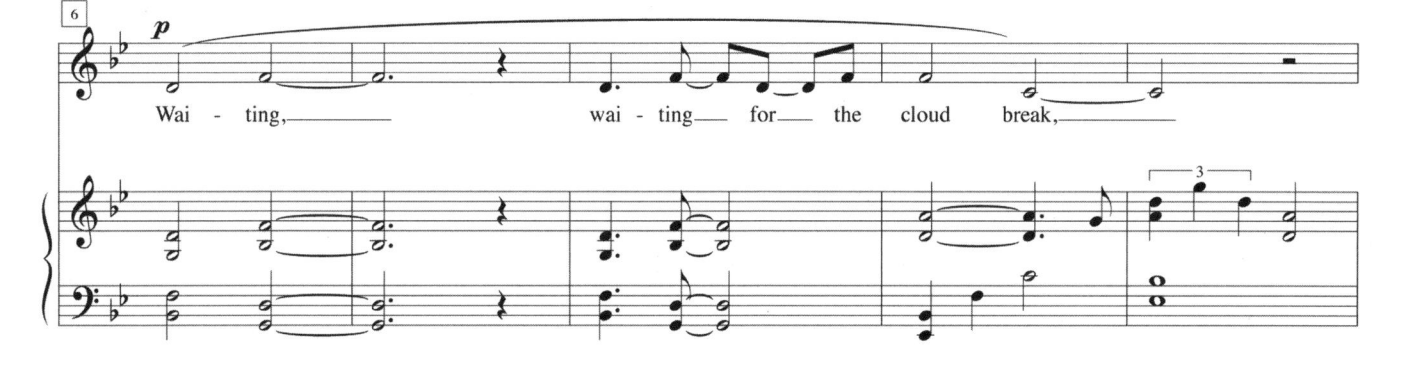

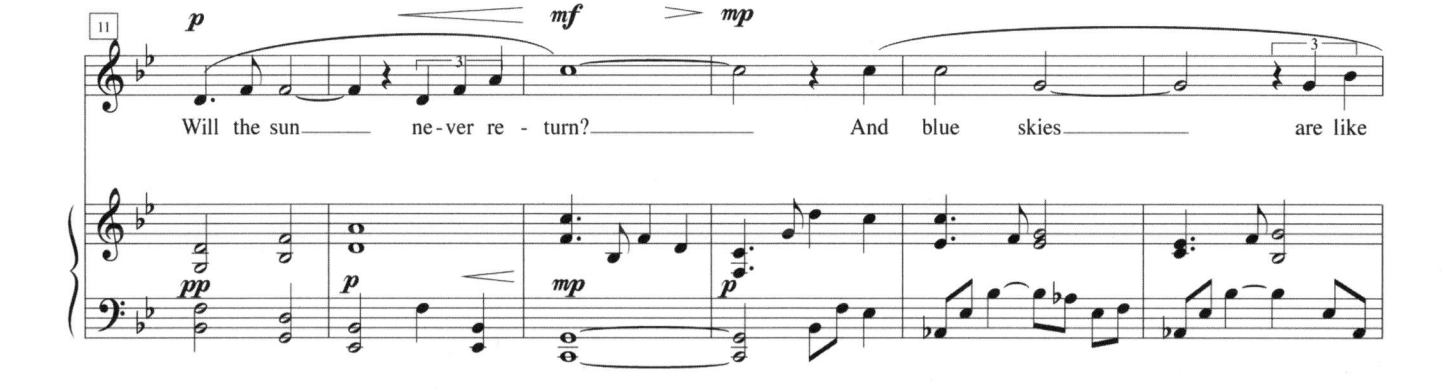

Wai - ting, _____ wai - ting for the cloud break, _____

Will the sun _____ ne-ver re - turn? _____ And blue skies _____ are like

rain - bows: _____ I on-ly see them _____ when there's hope. _____

Slightly Faster
22
mp
Time
p
Ped.
26
mf
mp
bub-bles on as the rain - drops make rip - ples on the
29
mf
f
side - - - walk. Ev - en the sha - dows hide
32
mp
p
when ev-ery-thing is grey.
decresc.

Tempo Primo
36
p
3
Fee - lings dull in the driz - zle, Com - pla-cen-cy
pp
Ped. ad lib.
42
2
set - tles in
p
Soft - ly, with-out a whis - per.
47
p mp pp
And I'm still wai - ting.
8va
3

# Waiting

*for high voice & piano*

Words & Music by
**WILLIAM CAMPBELL**

*Slow & Comfortable* (♩ = ca. 64)

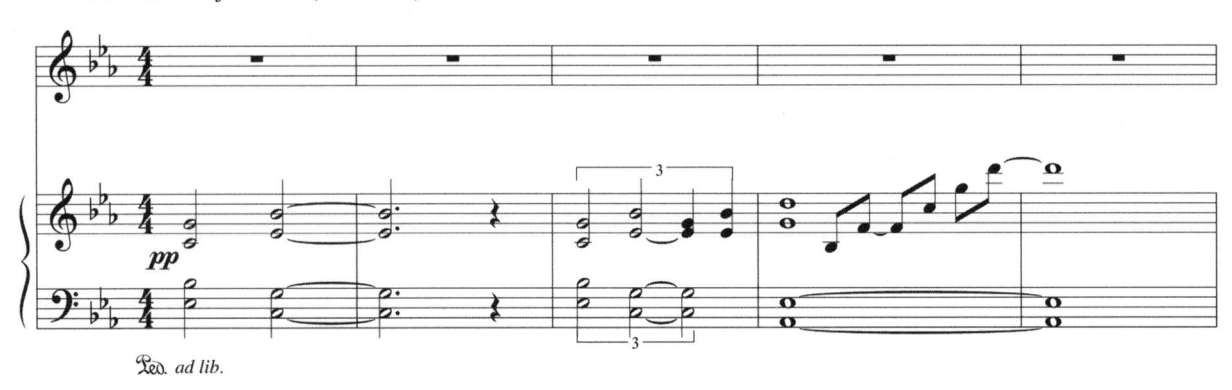

Wai - ting, _____ wai - ting for the cloud break, _____ Will the sun _____ ne - ver re - turn? _____ And blue skies _____ are like rain - bows: _____ I on - ly see them _____ when there's hope. _____

*Copyright © 1997 by William Campbell*
*www.WilliamCampbellMusic.com   All Rights Reserved*
**Used with Permission**

Slightly Faster
22
mp
Time
p
Ped.
26
mf
mp
bub-bles on as the rain - drops make rip - ples on the
29
mf
f
side - - - walk. Ev - en the sha - dows hide
32
mp
p
when ev-ery-thing is grey.
decresc.

Tempo Primo

Feelings dull in the drizzle, Complacency settles in

Softly, without a whisper.

And I'm still waiting.

# What can we poor females do

(come prima)
or com-ply-ing, But de-ny-ing or— com-ply-ing, What can we, what can we poor
(come prima)
fe-males do, When press-ing, teas-ing, press-ing, teas-ing lov-ers sue? What can we,—
what— can we— poor, poor— fe-males do? What can we,— what— can we—
poor, poor— fe-males do? And re-sent-ing, or con-sent-ing, And re-sent-ing,
or consent-ing Does a-like— our hopes be-tray,

(cresc. - -
What can we, what can we poor fe - males do, When press-ing, teas-ing,
(p) (strongly accented, non legato)
(cresc. - -
- - - - - - -)
press - ing, teas - ing lov - ers sue? What can we,— what— can we—
- - - - - - - -)
poor,— poor— fe - males do? What can we,— what— can we—
(simile)
(simile)
ritardando
poor, poor fe - males do?

# Erano i capei d'oro...

Francesco Petrarca
Alessandro Kirschner

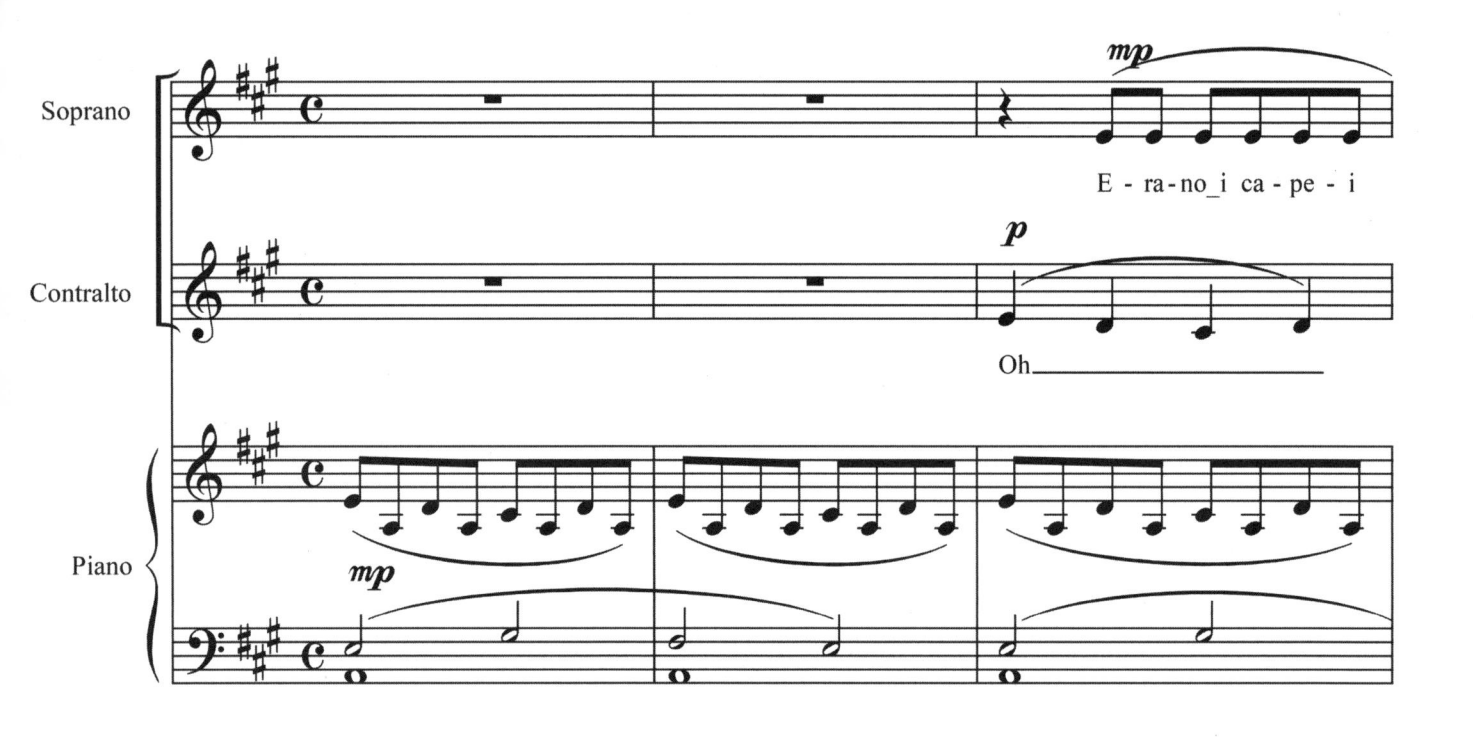

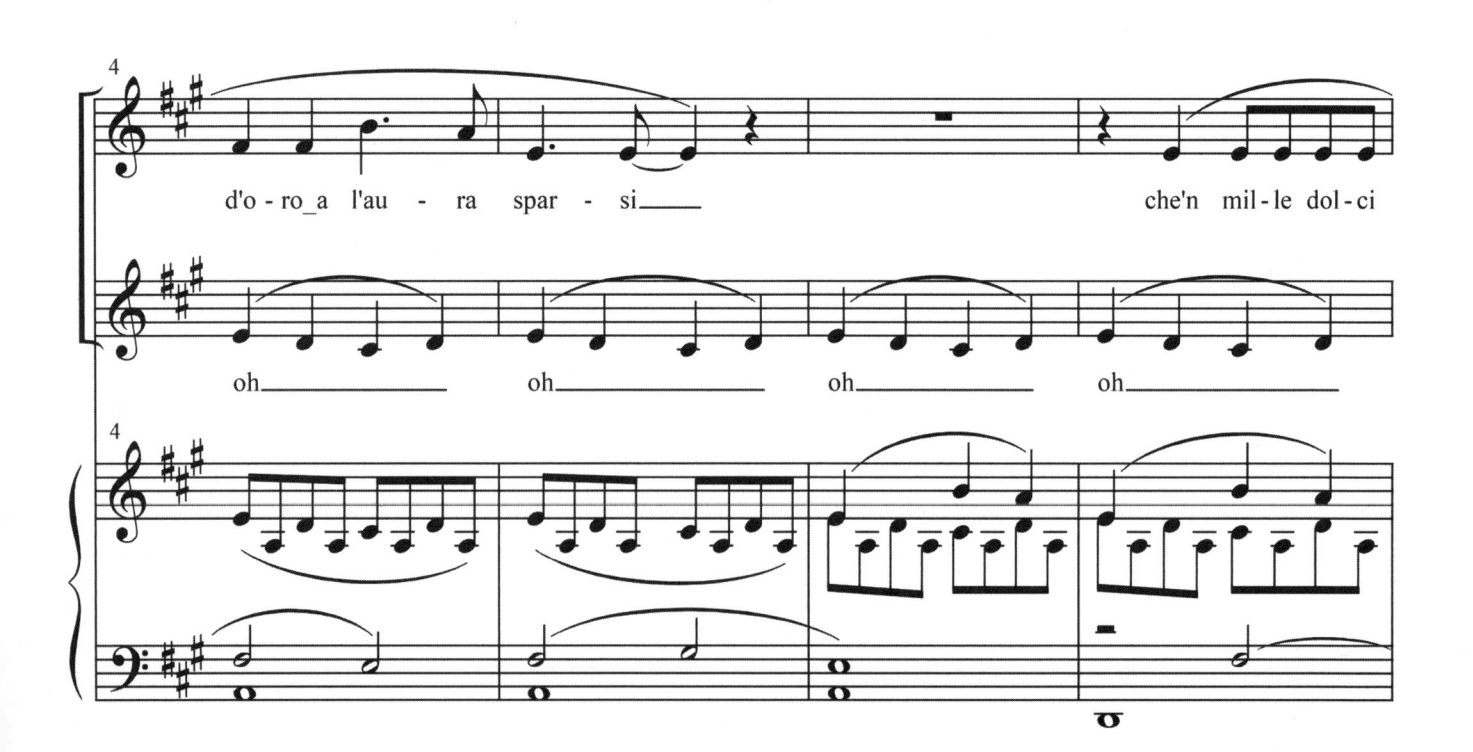

8
mf
no - di gli_av - vol - ge - a e_il va - go lu - me
mf
oh oh oh va - go lu - me
8
mf
12
ol - tre mi - su - ra_ar - de - a.
p
ol - tre mi - su - ra_ar - de - a va - go lu - me
12

e il viso di pie-
e quei be-glii oc-chi ch'or ne son si scar-si, oh___
to-si co-lor___ far-si___ non so se ve-ro_o
oh___ oh___ oh___ oh___

fal - so mi pa - re - a                    i' che l'e - sca

oh____ oh____ oh____ i'che che l'e - sca

a - mo - ro - sa in pet-to_a - ve - a.___

a - mo - ro - sa in pet-to_a - ve - a___ a - mo - ro - sa

Non qual meraviglia se di subito arsi.

Oh_____ oh_____ oh_____ ma d'angelica for-
e-ra l'andar su-o co-sa morta-le ma d'angelica for-

ma
e le pa-ro - le
so-na - van
ma
al - tro che pur vo-ce_u-ma - na.
U-no spr - to ce -
Oh

le - ste un v-vo so - le fu quel ch'i' vi - di e se non

oh oh fu quel ch'i' vi - di e se non

fos - se or ta - le pia - ga per al-len-tar

fos - se or ta - le

poco rall.
a tempo
50
d'ar - co non sa - na. Oh
mf
pp
pia - ga per al - len - tar d'ar - co non sa - na. Oh oh
54
oh
oh oh oh oh
poco rall.

# Mägdlein auf die Wiese gingen

Anton Rubenstein

Allegro

Soprano 1:
1. Mägd-lein auf die Wie-se gin-gen, Blu-men an zu pflü-cken fin-gen pflück-ten, ha-ben viel ge-fun-den
2. Lu-stig schmück-te ei-ne Dir-ne mit dem Kränz-lein ih-re Stir-ne, kei-ne geht nach Hau-se wie-der
3. Bö-se Hun-de bell-ten lan-gre und den Mägd-lein wur-de ban-ge, um die-sel-be Zeit zur Stun-de

Soprano 2:
1. Blu-men an zu pflü-cken fin-gen, pflück-ten, ha-ben viel ge-fun-den
2. Mit dem Kränz-lein ih-re Stir-ne, kei-ne geht nach Hau-se wie-der
3. Und den Mägd-lein wur-de ban-ge, um die-sel-be Zeit zur Stunde

und ein Kränz-lein draus ge-wun - - - - - den.
al - le sa-ßen mü-de nie - - - - - der.
kommt ein Jä-gers-mann ge-rit - - - - - ten.

und ein Kränz-lein draus ge-wun-den, draus ge-wun -
al - le sa-ßen mü-de nie-der, mü - - de nie -
kommt ein Jä-gers-mann ge-rit-ten, kommt ge-rit -

*cresc.*

4. Kommt ein Jä - gers-mann ge-rit - ten,

den.
der.
ten.

*f*

21
auf die Mägd - lein zu - ge - schrit - ten, gibt von sei ner
Auf die Mägd - lein zu - ge - schrit - ten, gibt von sei - ner
21
p
26
Lie - be Kun - de und ver - scheucht die bö - sen Hun - - - -
Lie - be Kun - de und ver - scheucht die bö - sen Hun - de, ja, die bö - sen
26
cresc.
f

de!

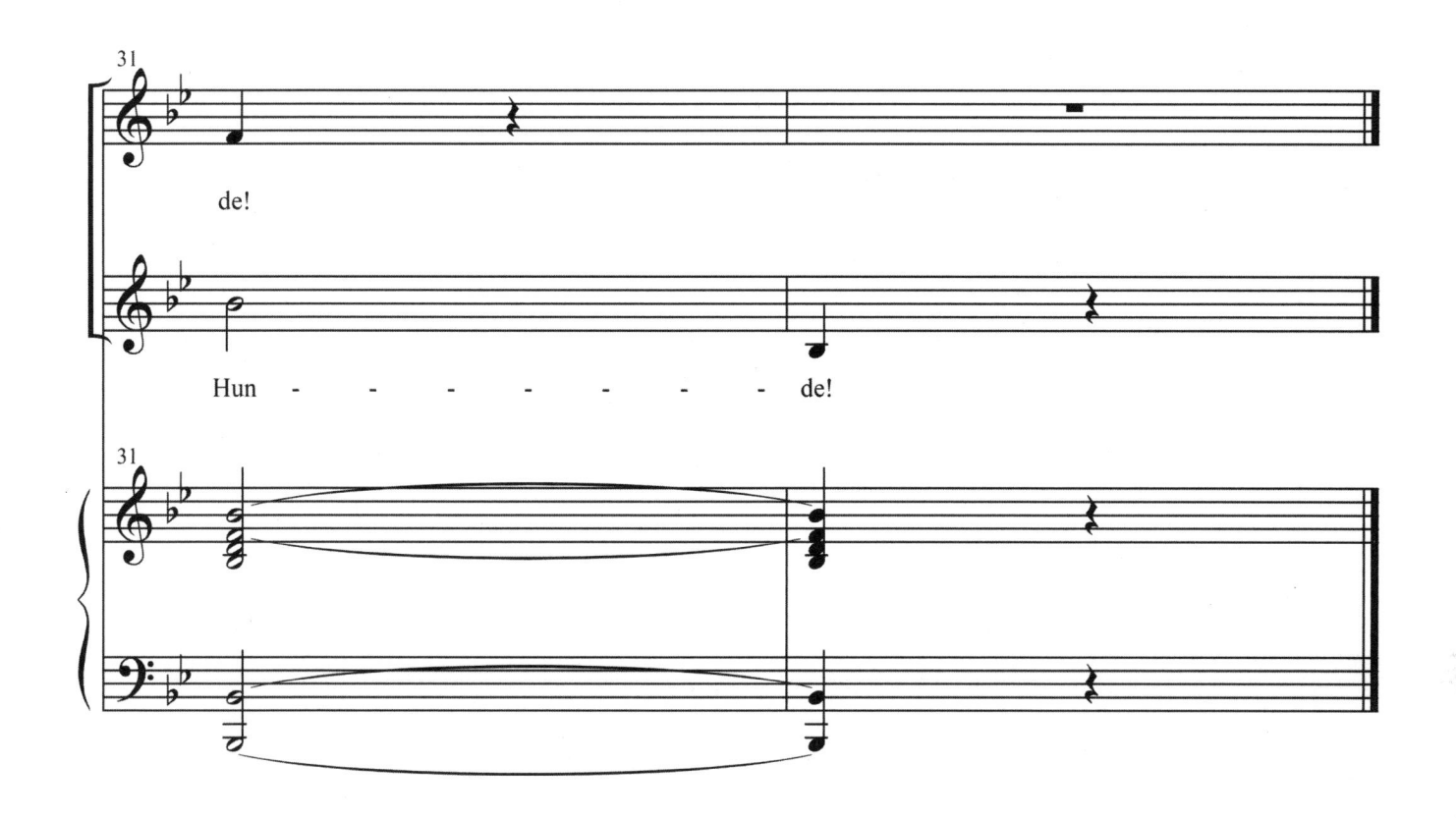

Hun - - - - - - de!

# My Dearest, My Fairest

attributed to Daniel or Henry Percell
edited by Marc Herouard

9
_ guish, I lan_____ guish, I lan_____
I lan_____ guish, I lan_____
9
13
_____ guish, I lan - guish for you. My
_____ guish, I lan - guish for you.
13
1.

17
2.
you. Thy kind - ness has won me,
2.
you. Thy charm has un -
17
2.
21
I ne'er no,
done me, I ne'er, I ne'er, I
21

ne'er shall be free.

ne'er, shall be free. I faint with the plea-sure I

Ah, why are love's rap-tures so fain would re-peat,

32
short and so___ sweet? Thus press___ ing,
And
32
35
thus press___ ing, and kiss___ ing, fresh
kiss___ ing, thus press___ ing and kiss___ ing fresh
35

38
joys we'll pur - sue, and e - ver be hap py, and
joys we'll pur - sue, and e - ver be hap py, and
38
42
e - ver be true, and e - ver be hap - py, and
e - ver be true, and e - ver be hap - py, and
42

46
e - ver be true. But a - las! should you change
e - ver be true. Ah,
46
50
No, ne - ver, my dear - est,
tell me not so No,
50

54
no, no
ne - ver, my fair - est, no, no,
54
57
no, no, no, no, no, no, my
no, no, no, no, no, no, no, my
57

61
dear est no, no! No, no,
fair est, no, no! No, no,
61
64
No, no, no, no, no,
no, no, no, no, no, no,
64

no,\_\_\_ my dear\_\_ est\_\_ no,\_\_ no!

no,\_\_\_ my fair\_\_ est,\_\_ no, no!

No,\_\_ no, no,\_\_\_ my\_\_ dear\_\_ est,\_\_ no,\_\_ no!

No,\_\_ no, no,\_\_ my\_\_ fair\_\_ est,\_\_ no, no!

# Wanderers Nachtlied

(Lermontoff)

Anton Rubenstein

197

dunk - ler Nacht, al - ler Bäu - me Wip - - fel

ruhn in dunk - ler Nacht, al - ler Bäu - me Wip - fel

ruhn,_____ kein Vög - lein wacht; rauscht kein Blatt im

ruhn,_____ kein Vög - lein wacht; rauscht kein

*p*

20
Wal - de ü - ber - all ist Ruh,
Blatt im Wal - de, ü - ber - all ist Ruh,
20
23
war - ter, Wand - rer bal - de, bal - de ruhst auch
war - te, Wand - rer bal - de bal - de ruhst auch
23
mf
pp

du, warte, Wandrer bal - - - de,
du, warte, Wandrer bal - de,

bal - de ruhst auch du!
bal - de ruhst auch du!

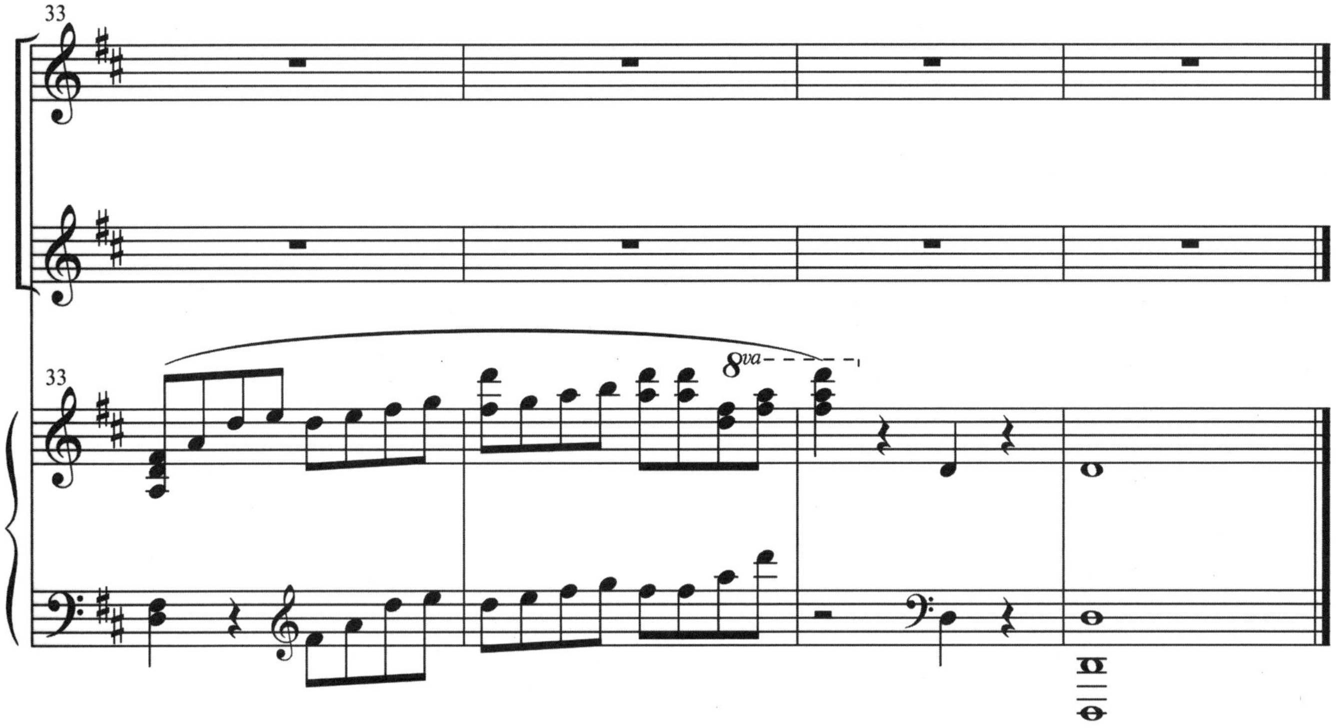
33
33
8va

# Part III

# Teacher's Guide

**What is an Aging Singer?**

The definitions of aging singers are as varied as the terminology used to describe them. In my work with these singers, they have called themselves "mature" singers, older adult singers, aging singers, and even old-people singers. Further description and explanation is needed to make distinctions among all these students of singing. This book, however, focuses specifically on the complex issues relevant to aging *amateur* singers.

In all of my research and presentations, I have referred to an **aging singer** as someone 60 years or older who enjoys singing in groups or as a soloist, usually in church or community chorus situations. Laura Berk, in her textbook, *Development Through the Lifespan*, defines late adulthood as age 65 to the end of the lifespan (562). This closely corresponds to the definition I have described above. By no means are we discussing the needs of aging professional singers, nor will we attempt to turn aging voices into professional quality instruments. Rather, we will examine the characteristics and needs of this large student population whom we encounter as voice teachers and choir directors.

My categorization of aging singers is based on students I have had in class or lessons or have observed in church choirs. These categories primarily are based on level of involvement in singing and past musical training. **"Lifers,"** for example, are people who sing regularly, at least once a week in a formal ensemble, such as church choir or community chorus. They are the regulars, who have sung in these situations for many years and for whom the thought of ceasing this activity is not acceptable. They also may have enhanced their musical experiences by participating in community musical theater, a barbershop or "beauty shop" (e.g. Sweet Adelines) chorus or quartet, and may have sung as a soloist in church or with a big band. More often than not, they have had voice lessons in the past, but may not actively be engaged in that pursuit at the moment. They understand the basics of singing but are open to learning more about their individual instruments and bodies, and discovering or rediscovering cherished vocal literature. One of my most recent students grew up singing hymns at church, took voice lessons in college, and sang solos in informal recitals with his pianist wife. At the age of 84, he is still active in his church choir and enjoys bringing music from his past to our class. He definitely is a "Lifer."

**"Groupies"** (pun intended) are aging singers who participate in vocal music enterprises through a church or community musical organization, but are not experienced or necessarily comfortable with solo singing. Most often, participation in vocal music has not been a central part of their lives; they might have joined and rejoined ensembles as their schedules allowed. They usually never have taken voice lessons and therefore have a limited understanding of their instruments. They present with no debilitating vocal habits and are able to explore their vocal potential quite easily. My most recent example of a "groupie" is a pair of sisters who joined my class in order to return to singing duets together. Both sing in a church choir and have a history of singing in quartets with their brothers. Neither has any vocal dysfunction, but they need additional information about techniques for breathing, proper vowel resonance, and details of the singing process.

The **"Wounded Warbler"** is a third category of aging singers with varying amounts of participation in singing, but who now have some type of vocal dysfunction. Most often, phrasing, tuning and vibrato are the most significant problems. They may have been absent from vocal enterprises for quite some time because of their vocal problems, but they generally miss these experiences and are seeking ways to rejoin them. These are the most challenging students with whom we work. But when each particular dysfunction is understood and time and patience are applied, they generally find ways to work around the dysfunction. I have encountered both male and female singers in this category who have vibrato problems. Each has focused on healthy breathing and resonance techniques and has managed to make progress, despite the inability to turn back the clock. Finding appropriate literature also has helped, as has increasing their basic understanding of the singing process.

We should not forget those singers that I call **"Explorers."** These people are quite inexperienced as singers, having had no formal vocal training and no consistent participation in vocal enterprises. They may or may not have been professional voice users, such as pastors or teachers, but they have little or no understanding of their instrument. They simply are curious learners. These singers are some of the most enjoyable because they possess so many characteristics of committed lifelong learners. One student I encountered in an early voice class was so intrigued by the process of singing that he joined the local town and gown choir and began taking private voice lessons. He is a classic example of an Explorer.

Figure 1. Continuum of Singing Activity.
Least active to Most Active

Of course there are singers who do not fall cleanly into these categories. Trends in participation and experience can be clues to vocal problems and/or the raw material with which voice teachers and choir directors must work. Knowing our students' background, knowledge, motivation, and any hindrances to their development can help us make their learning more efficient and successful.

### What can Aging Singers do for Voice Teachers and Choir Directors?

The relationship between aging singers and their teachers is not one-sided, with aging singers receiving all of the benefits. This population can increase a teacher's pool of students, making a positive impact on his income and influence in the community. Teachers then are able to increase the understanding of vocal concepts for more students, producing better-informed singers who contribute more positively to solo and group vocal efforts. These students also provide satisfying teaching experiences. They are interesting people with a wealth of history and experience to share, and in general are highly committed because they are self-motivated to study, not forced by parents or others who think taking a lesson or a class is a good idea.

Teachers also broaden their own contributions to community musical experiences when they have more students to draw from for a wide variety of performances, such as singing the national anthem at a local baseball game or putting a group together to sing at local nursing homes. All of these benefits are a result of mutual efforts to enjoy the study and teaching of singing and are a tribute to the value found in working with older adults.

### What can Teachers do for Aging Singers?

To be most effective, teachers need a broad understanding of the many changes experienced by older adults during the aging process. Anatomic and physiologic, as well as psychosocial and cognitive changes are many and varied in aging singers. But understanding how these adults are influenced to think and act in learning and social situations allows teachers to identify problems quickly and to find appropriate solutions. A choir director can facilitate retention by presenting information within a specific context. For example, she can help to ensure that desired breathing and phrasing is retained from rehearsal to rehearsal by writing them into the musical score (which also helps to reduce frustration caused by choir members who can't remember instructions from week to week). Because aging singers have varied life experience, health status and motivation, it is necessary for teachers to understand age-related changes to the instrument, body, and mind, to enhance each student's musical experience.

Anatomic and physiologic changes to the body and larynx can lead to decreased vocal ability and increased frustration for many aging singers. Robert Sataloff states that age-related changes to the voice generally are caused by lessened neurologic function, loss of muscle bulk and elasticity, decreased respiratory function and blood flow, and ossification of cartilages (20).

Figure 2. Relationship of Changes in the Aging Process.

Difficulty maintaining breath through long phrases, instability of pitch, and declining posture are just a few of the problems that aging singers face. It is important to know that "many of these acoustic phenomena are not caused by irreversible age changes. Rather, they may be consequences of poor laryngeal, respiratory, and abdominal muscle condition, which undermines the power source of the voice" (Sataloff, 34).

**What changes do we need to consider?**

So with what changes, exactly, must older adults cope? Changes in social roles and groups, information processing, problem solving and memory, as well as learning goals and attitudes toward learning are important components of life-cycle changes. We commonly think of these as changes in psychosocial behavior and cognitive function.

Despite the effects of the aging process on singing abilities, many people stay involved in group music-making not only for the musical experience, but also to maintain social contacts. Imagine a widower who attended choir rehearsals with his wife. Her passing and his avoidance of reminders of her presence could create a void in his social interactions. But if he maintains his membership in a choir, he maintains his interactions with others and decreases the possibility that a loss of role, social isolation and/or marginalization will occur (Brandtstädter 124).

It is important that teachers remember the social function of their organizations and allow for those moments as well. They need to comprehend the impact of changing social and personal roles on involvement, comprehension, and commitment while recognizing that these factors affect older adults at different rates and to varying degrees. For teachers, the result of dealing with multiple changes to the body and psyche of older adults is a renewed focus on establishing and maintaining the coping mechanisms that work for each student's unique situation. In other words, finding ways for singers to reminisce during a lesson, through choice of literature or conversation, allows them to cope with the loss of significant others and feelings of aloneness. Keeping them connected to friends and acquaintances provides a diversion from the painful reminders of a loved-one's absence. These social dimensions of interpersonal connection easily can be facilitated by voice teachers and choir directors.

Changes in roles, isolation and depression are significant issues with which some older adults must deal during the aging process. Some have difficulty transitioning from work to retirement; some have significant health issues that impact the frequency of their participation in activities. Others experience a loss of direction and connection when the patterns of living they have known for decades are changed by life circumstances. Consider a student whom I will call George. George is an elderly man who recently lost his wife, moved from the independence of his own home, and is now living with his son and family. Singing in choir and voice class helped him transition through these changes, allowing him to connect with other people with similar interests. He has remained involved in making music, an activity he loves. Voice teachers and choir directors who are open to the contributions George can make will be providing a valuable service to him and to others in similar situations, helping to combat loneliness and depression.

Signs of changes in cognition can occur before the age of 65; for our student George, they have created significant frustration. A longtime lover of music, George would be classified as a "Lifer." He sang in choirs throughout his life, took voice lessons in college, sang in informal recitals with his wife, sang for his school students as their principal, and continues to sing in his church choir. At the age of 84, he is frustrated with the difficulty he faces singing high notes that once were easy, the increased effort it takes to sing long phrases, and his general lack of stamina. However, George still has a sense of humor through which he filters his understanding and emotions, and maintains a positive attitude toward singing and learning. While he still has much of his vocal prowess intact, the changes he is experiencing started more than 20 years ago. For example, the nervous system that is involved in processing information slows down; in other words, it takes longer for information to be processed (Berk 518). In addition, some adults find it more difficult to pay attention to multiple stimuli, and their resistance to distraction and memory abilities decreases as well (Berk 519). George not only has to deal with a body that is changing, but a mind that is changing too. With all of these things impacting an older adult, it is no wonder that instructions must be repeated more often than one would expect, or that the pace of change in singing behaviors is slower. Despite this, older adults become more efficient with practical problem solving, rather than abstract or complex instructions (Berk 520). This means that complex information breeds repetition, but simple or practical information enables efficiency and retention.

Research has found that as adults move from middle to late adulthood (into their 60s), their ability to recall information from long-term memory declines (Berk 588). This is partly because in late adulthood there is reduced perception about a given stimulus and its context. In other words, there are fewer reference points for the memory, which makes it more difficult to recall. To combat this tendency, when working on expressive devices, such as crescendos, have students find ways to expand the relevant context. Have them examine the text, provide its meaning, analyze the musical phrase and try to suggest the reason a composer chose those musical elements in that particular order, so that a context for the devices can be established. That broader context is the reference point and the reminder to execute a crescendo the next time they sing that phrase. A reminder of the context or reference point then replaces repetition of instruction from lesson to lesson or rehearsal to rehearsal.

There also appears to be a deficit in associative memory, or creating and retrieving links between pieces of information (Berk 588). This can be managed by providing devices to record a reference point for future recall. Devices such as a song worksheet or checklist of items to review before each performance of a song, or a handout with specific vocalises for students to practice on their own are just a few of the ways students can be reminded of the links between concepts that affect their vocal output.

The need to balance this decrease of memory in older adults with the abilities of younger singers in a group situation may dictate particular teaching methods in rehearsal. If those differences go unaddressed, frustration for the uninformed or insensitive teacher or fellow ensemble member increases, leading to decreased morale and reduced enjoyment in the music-making experience for everyone. Research by Erber and Prager has shown that this is because people who are observed making memory mistakes are seen as less capable (197). The resulting negative stigma associated with memory lapses can be so disconcerting for aging singers that it causes them to withdraw prematurely from the activity.

Voice teachers and choir directors easily and erroneously can believe that older singers are less capable, especially if they continually must remind them about artistic elements, such as phrasing and dynamics for a particular piece of music. In this circumstance, however, it should be noted that it is not the actual memory lapse that matters, but rather, how that adult handles the memory failure. If she sees it for what it is, a simple memory lapse, it does not become debilitating. But if the students try to cover it up, or a teacher mistakenly tries to help them cope by making an excuse for it, they run the risk of utilizing unhealthy coping mechanisms that can lead to isolation and depression, or a loss of interest in things that stimulate their lives. Teachers can better assist these older adults by not focusing on the repetition of instruction that occurs, but rather finding teaching methods that help to minimize that repetition, such as those described above.

When it comes to learning, voice teachers and choir directors would be mistaken if they believed the phrase, "you can't teach an old dog new tricks." A more comprehensive understanding of the needs of adult learners negates this saying. If learning opportunities are structured appropriately, older adults *can* learn and grow. Several researchers have documented factors that impact adult learning.

K. Patricia Cross has thoroughly considered the needs of adult learners. She notes that previous educational experiences play a large role in how well someone will learn in a new situation, stating that many times "learning is addictive; the more education people have, the more they want, and the more they will get" (Cross 55). I have encountered such addictive behavior with my voice class participants; everyone who has been involved for more than one year had previously attended some institution of higher education and usually was involved in musical activities. Many have been "Lifers," but the "Explorers" are wonderful examples of what Cross talks about: pupils who are addicted to learning. They exhibit an approach that many of us wish our young learners would exhibit: a continuous curiosity about singing. They are intrigued and approach each session as if it were a class for college credit. Many are ready with questions and make connections between what they experience in our voice class and what they experience in their choral or solo singing situations. Those who have not returned to voice class were less interested in the depth of knowledge they could gain and more interested in quick fixes for their singing problems. These same students also lacked confidence or were affected by issues of decreased mobility or serious cognitive changes that made learning more difficult (Cross 58).

Another concern about learning in this student population is that older adults can have difficulty retrieving words (Berk 590). This manifests itself in a slow rate of speech or hesitations as they plan what to say. Both situations can limit participation in learning activities. Students are frustrated with themselves, and teachers can be impatient, sending signals to the student of annoyance. There also can be generational influence at play in these situations. Other authors have noted interesting distinctions between adult learners and younger students. For instance, Lenz found that adult learners are self-directed versus dependent and use their experience and motivation as a primary learning resource. They are problem-oriented (24); if they are having trouble singing particular high or low notes, they will learn best when they are focused on fixing that problem. They will learn well with shorter and lively "lecture" sessions (10-15 minutes), and when they are taught through multiple learning styles. Recognizing these differences and allowing for understanding of any communication issues will lessen the possibility of negative interactions.

But in the absence of such problems and regardless of any natural affinity for learning, what else motivates older adults to learn? Further research identifies some of these motivators. It may seem obvious, but studies of participants in adult education found that high-learning older adults (1,121 hours of independent learning in 1 year) were motivated by psychological need; low learners (<100 hours) were crisis driven. High learners saw themselves as "reliable, tenacious, independent, having broad interests, high achievement motivations, and open to new experiences" (Armstrong). Here we see the manifestation of some successful use of the coping mechanisms previously identified. These learners see themselves as being and behaving the way they want to, as looking toward the future and not limited by the aging process. These have been the participants I have encountered in my voice classes. Contrastingly, low learners see themselves as "warm and friendly, masculine, conformist, and either complacently satisfied or angrily resigned to their current life situations" (Armstrong 66). These learners are the ones who do not come back to the class or quit their musical commitments prematurely.

Cross suggests that to keep this type of learner involved, we need to raise confidence levels by presenting activities with low levels of initial risk (Cross 133). One way to do this is to recreate the learning experience to feel less like a class, even if it is organized that way. This means decreasing formality and using appropriate teaching techniques. Berk notes that older adults often feel self-conscious in classroom settings, but that these feelings can be overcome by using appropriate teaching techniques (Berk 523). For example, asking students to sing in groups rather than by themselves in a voice class or ensemble situation decreases risk. They do not risk having flaws in their vocal tone identified as readily in such a situation and feel less self-conscious.

Once we understand why adults engage in learning, we can begin to identify the kinds of knowledge they best retain and tailor our teaching in that direction. One author notes that there is an increase in the "breadth and depth of practical knowledge" in the adult learner, which means, the less abstract the concept, the more that knowledge will be retained. I remember trying to explain resonance during one voice class. Dissecting the science of acoustics into relevant information is difficult, and on this occasion, I did not simplify the concepts sufficiently, which thoroughly confused my adult class members. A basic explanation that efficient resonance makes singing easier and that vowel production plays a part in what we hear might have been enough. Teachers must remind themselves that simplifying teaching leads to better retention of information. Also, despite issues with memory loss, older adult reasoning ability *does not decrease*, so we must not believe that they cannot learn new ways of looking at situations (Lenz 89). This means that when we explain a concept, they will understand it, but they might not remember how to apply the knowledge without proper memory prompts or repetition.

These facts about learning highlight the benefits of older adult involvement in studying singing. If they participate in choral ensembles or have an outlet as a soloist, they automatically have places in which to apply the practical information received in the rehearsal or studio lesson. Having an outlet means they can retain the information better and put it to good use, which ensures better vocal output for an ensemble. Teachers must consider our focused work with older adults as having a benefit to communal and solo singing and as teaching for lifelong learning. Berk cites several benefits: new knowledge, new friends, new perspectives, and intergenerational contact, which leads to a decline in stereotyping (Berk 525). If we truly are going to influence quality of life for aging singers, voice teachers and choir directors must be partners with all students, helping them to negotiate the physical and psychological changes of older adulthood.

**Coping with Change**

It is safe to assume that all of these changes create much frustration for older adults. Research supports that notion, telling us that when older adults are questioned about aging, they say that the negatives of the process seem to outweigh the positives. "People feel that they drift away from their desired self in many attributes, and this negative tendency increases with age" (Brandstädter 124). So how are we to help them transition to and through this process? I believe the answer lies in being informed, prepared, and compassionate. One way to facilitate understanding is by defining and identifying coping mechanisms. Our work intersects with these coping mechanisms because making music serves this very purpose for many aging singers.

Researchers in the field of social cognition have developed categories of coping mechanisms for use in understanding how older adults deal with memory losses and life changes. These same researchers acknowledge the common perception that older adults experience depression and hopelessness when they encounter a loss of function or a significant life change. Some researchers work from the premise that gains and losses in function are not bad in and of themselves, but rather it is how those gains and losses relate to people's goals, preferences, and self-definitions that has the most impact on depression or hopelessness. The most significant factor in determining how individuals cope with change is the level of discrepancy between who they are and who they want to be, or how they function and how they want to function. Depression and hopelessness are most likely to occur when people think they cannot become what they want to be (Brandstädter 126). This is where singing teachers can step in to become facilitators of healthy coping. They can provide solutions for changes in vocal function and encourage singers to stay in choir, try a new musical group, or simply pay special attention to the singer's situation so that he knows his contributions are valued.

Teachers can best assist in this process by understanding specific coping mechanisms that students might exhibit. Brandstädter & Greve provide helpful definitions of assimilative, accommodative, and immunizing modes of coping. **Assimilative** coping is when the behavior or self is the object of correction. This most often is the case when coping with changes to the larynx and the singing voice. Taking lessons and trying to improve are assimilative techniques. **Accommodative** coping is an attempt to alter the individual's evaluation of the problem, rather than the situation itself. This is exemplified by older adults finding excuses for a breathy tone, such as blaming it on allergies instead of decreased respiratory function or inefficient glottal closure. Finally, the **immunizing** mode is when a person does not look at the self-discrepancies, but tries to enhance his or her sense of self and acts in a self-serving manner (Brandtstädter et al 126). This kind of coping most commonly is seen in an aging singer who tries to continue as a soloist in church, despite the fact that his solo voice is compromised by the aging process and has not been retrained or recently instructed.

It is important to understand that these modes are not necessarily mutually exclusive; they can work synergistically, but tend to inhibit each other when used in such a manner (Brandtstädter et al 126). Ignoring problems in immunizing mode works against improvement of technical singing skill, which is the object of the corrections made in assimilative coping. For students, it is more effective to commit to changing one's situation or how it is evaluated, rather than to believe that nothing is wrong or nothing needs to change. Kind conversation is a teacher's best tool for addressing such a situation. Recognizing that a student is unwilling or emotionally unable to change, and working within that resistance also is important. This type of situation has played out for me several times when teaching older adults. I have had singers who want to improve a skill such as resonance, but believe that it is better to use a quiet, disconnected, breathy tone that might blend better in choir. In this situation, letting the singer know she has personal control over how she accommodates her changing vocal function provides a more successful teaching strategy than pointing out the consequences of poor vocal choices (e.g. muscle strain and vocal fatigue). Like anything, too little personal control leads to depression and defeat, while too much control leads to decreased flexibility in redefining goals. Flexibility with accommodation helps us become more resilient as we age (Brandtstädter 133).

Another important component of any coping mechanism is the ability to look toward the future. However, if that forward view is not realistic, it can increase one's susceptibility to depression and alienation in later life (Brandtstädter 135). Realistic goals appear to be the key to making effective use of this aspect of coping. For the older adult, goals that are timeless may be more important than goals based on a particular timetable. A realistic goal in this manner might be deciding phrasing abilities or breathing techniques will improve in each song that is sung, rather than deciding that all phrasing problems will be resolved in two months.

Vocal practitioners can be of great service in articulating realistic goals for their choir members or studio singers. They can facilitate the coping mechanisms described above and protect the elderly from negative, age-based stereotypes, giving them the best opportunity for successful negotiation of life cycle changes (Brandtstädter 136).

## How do we get Started?

This section will help the singing teacher and choir director implement approaches to teaching older adults that have proven effective in studio, class, and choral situations. From self-assessment, to implementation, the path to success and satisfaction from teaching older adults can seem complicated, but easily is within one's grasp.

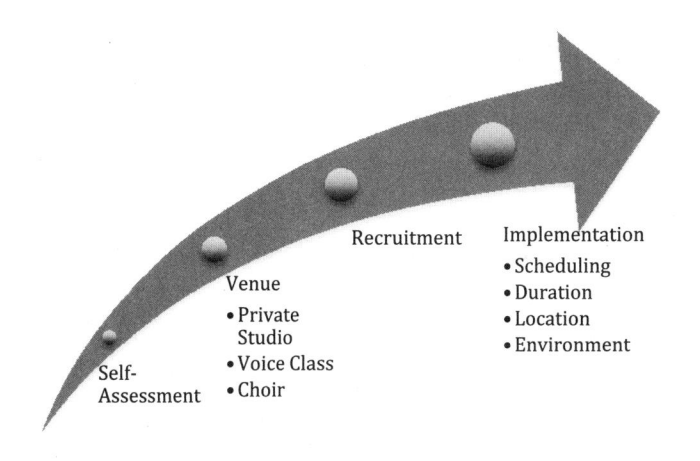

Figure 3. Pathway to Teaching Older Adults

## Self-Assessment

First and foremost, teachers realistically need to consider their preparation for teaching older adults in an appropriate manner. Preparation refers to all applicable information that teachers currently possess about working with older adults, and their confidence in applying that information. Many choir directors are not given a choice regarding the ages of singers in their ensembles, especially in the case of church choirs. But when a choice can be made, such as developing an applied singing studio that invites older adults, teachers should seriously consider whether working with this student population is a good personal choice. Balancing the needs, challenges and goals of each student with the gifts, talents and goals of the teacher is an essential step in preparation. It is advisable that teachers ensure they can be committed to these students and have a proper understanding of their instruments.

Once a teacher has decided to work with older adults, the format or venue must thoroughly be examined before recruitment of students and teaching can commence. There are three primary venues for teaching singing concepts to older adults: individual singing lessons, voice class, and choirs.

**One-on-one singing lessons**

Studio teaching typically involves 30-45 minute lessons on a weekly or biweekly basis. For many teachers and older adult students, this provides ample time to address technical and expressive issues without creating fatigue, and permits uninterrupted attention to a singer's unique vocal needs. The lesson can be filled quickly with casual conversation, which is certainly appropriate and expected in a teacher/student relationship that functions as social interaction as well as musical training; therefore, teachers might try to minimize time constraints on either side of a lesson with older adults so they do not perceive they are a bother or annoyance. In my experience, teaching older adults in this format has been a delightful challenge; my pace can slow to accommodate theirs, which has been refreshing. The lessons I teach generally are structured the same as for my other students, with time for vocalizing and song literature.

**Voice Class**

A voice class is a unique setting that can be led either by a choral director or a voice teacher who understands and implements the format appropriately. It usually is a weekly one hour to one and a half hour class of 6-10 people who sing in groups for vocal warm-ups and then as soloists or in small groups for vocal literature, through which technical and expressive skills are developed. There usually is a time for questions and in-depth study of some aspect of singing, when singers can double-check their understanding of what they are doing in their choral ensembles and have the opportunity for direct, individual feedback. For some participants, it also increases the frequency of singing opportunities that keep them involved in the process and more physically prepared for what is required.

This format has unique benefits for the aging singer/student population. First and foremost, it provides a venue for addressing specific needs of aging singers on a very personal level. Singers are grouped with others who are experiencing the same changes and therefore are more likely to take risks to discover their vocal potential. Participants are able to train their ears to hear positive and negative vocal output while exchanging feedback with their peers. These ideas are supported by Baroody and Smith, who point out that singing in groups is helpful for older people because they are together with those who face similar life changes (Sataloff 61). They are less self-conscious and feel free to make mistakes because those listening likely will make the same mistakes. As one of my participants pointed out, "Class is a way of meeting people of similar interest and [vocal] hardships."

Voice class allows teachers to do what Lenz suggests by providing a "noncompetitive environment where there can be social interaction." Having a voice class not only creates a safe environment for learning and taking risks, but also a supportive environment where singers receive valuable feedback from their classmates. My participants have noted that, "...we noticed voice improvements. We also thought that listening to our own sounds has been important." Listening in a small group setting is easier and provides immediate and specific feedback to its participants, rather than the generalized feedback to voice parts that can occur in choir rehearsals or the one-sided critique of a one-on-one voice lesson.

Another benefit of voice class is that it can be conveniently scheduled to meet the needs of the teacher and students because many older singers are retired and have flexible time for such activities. Many times, independent teachers deal with after-school scheduling for their younger studio members, many of whom are still enrolled in high school or middle school. And while choir directors normally might find it difficult to make time for sectionals, a voice class can address a core group of singers in a consistent manner. Participants in a collaborative voice class had the following to say about the experience:

> "I really like the class aspect of studying voice. Our class is so very supportive of everyone. It is a wonderful atmosphere under which to perform."

> "Personally, I have found a greater appreciation of breath support, and by active practicing I have started to breathe more correctly without having to concentrate on it. I realize that daily breath and vocal exercises are just as important as physical exercises for the body and voice. I believe I am more aware of all aspects of performance: mental preparation, physical preparation/exercise, and vocal preparation. I have a greater understanding of the mechanics of singing, and where I am in regard to the different areas of preparation and performance. All in all, I believe I have greatly benefited by these sessions and I hope to participate in the next session."

Others noted benefits such as having better experiences as a church soloist and more satisfying participation in the community chorus "Messiah" performance.

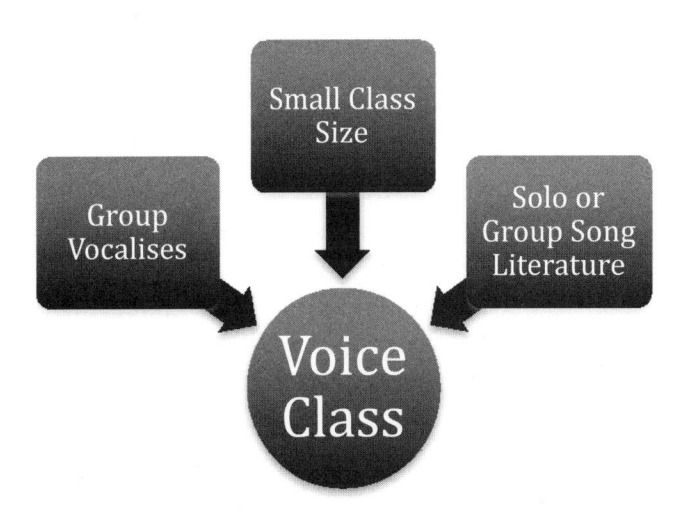

Figure 4. Elements of Voice Class

### Choir

The choir rehearsal is a teaching venue that needs to accomplish many goals at once. Learning music, language pronunciation, and singing expressively and healthfully are all part of a typical one or two hour weekly rehearsal. This reality presents unique challenges to the aging singer and may seem beyond the control of the director. Challenges posed by time and length of the rehearsal, its location, and the learning environment may be unavoidable, but not insurmountable. If the choir rehearsal is the only format a director has to offer advice for aging singers, she can focus on breathing and resonance techniques that will maximize individual contributions and minimize disturbances to the desired choral sound. For example, my colleagues frequently concentrate on breath use when working with aging singers in their community choirs. Reminders of how to breathe, how to stay relaxed and how to use air are appropriate for maximizing the potential of singers in a choral environment. Acknowledgment of what can and can't be accomplished during a choral rehearsal is important for both the director and voice teacher to remember as each new situation is encountered.

## Other options

Sometimes choir directors cannot accomplish all their goals in one rehearsal with aging singers. In these cases, they should consider collaborating with knowledgeable voice teachers or offer a voice class or lessons themselves, if they are qualified to do so. The point is to offer as many opportunities for maintenance and growth to aging singers as is possible. By singing more frequently, these adults have more chances to implement proper vocal techniques and to avoid falling into bad habits.

Some directors work with ensembles of mixed ages and encounter interesting interpersonal dynamics within the rehearsal environment. Motivation, concentration, and goals may vary widely between generations, causing some angst. Voice classes tailored to specific age groups can combat this dynamic and bring all members of the larger ensemble to more common ground. On the other hand, sometimes those involved in voice class become quite critical of other singers in the choir who do not seem to be responding in ways the director asks. Singers who participate in voice class are better informed vocally and become more intelligent singers, consequently seeking a higher standard of excellence from their peers, no matter what their age. This desire for excellence is something that we can assume most directors and teachers are striving to harness or establish within each student or chorister; its emphasis through specialized classes aids in pursuit of that goal.

Another benefit of connecting with a voice teacher is that issues specific to the solo voice can be addressed in greater depth. Many of the singers I have had in class primarily think of themselves as ensemble singers and may never have given any thought to their solo voice or to any solo singing opportunities. However, once they join the class and move past singing with others in a group setting to singing solos, they begin to see realistic possibilities for themselves. One singer in her 60's noted in her journal: "My daughter invited me for lunch and I took my CD and sang her my song. I would never have done that before being in this class! She thought I was much improved." This same singer also said, "I had an idea (while I was warming up)...one that would never have occurred to me before lessons. Maybe I could give a recital at my mom's nursing home. There are only 20-25 residents and they all know me. They certainly would be an appreciative audience." These comments show that for some older adults, having the opportunity to focus on and learn about their voices provides new opportunities for growth and facilitates lifelong learning and life satisfaction.

Collaboration on this kind of learning opportunity can be beneficial for the voice teacher as well. As previously mentioned, voice classes for singers over 60 can be offered during the day, avoiding afternoon scheduling conflicts with school aged voice students. A class offering such as this also can be viewed as community service or community outreach by those teachers who want to ensure they are contributing in this manner.

The choir director who does not have a voice teacher available to assist in the training of aging singers might establish a class on her own. Through small-group and one-on-one contact, the director ends up knowing her singers extremely well and can more effectively choose music, structure rehearsals and create art through the ensemble. It is therefore essential that this person understands the vocal mechanism and the developmental changes that take place in later adulthood.

## Recruitment

Many voice teachers and choir directors have mechanisms built into their organizational frameworks that make recruitment of older students quite easy, such as connections to a church or school. However, when establishing a voice class, it is important to consider what avenues are open to locating a base of students with whom to work. I personally have recruited at senior centers, including those with choral groups for retirees, community choirs such as "town-and-gown" (local and campus communities) masterworks choruses, and through church music directors. All have proved helpful in adding students to the class and refreshing the membership. Current students often will bring curious friends to the class. Teachers should be open and willing to work with these guest students, who can be wonderful additions to the class. Maintaining interest in the class after recruitment depends heavily on how each teacher implements strategies that take aging singers into consideration.

**Implementation**

In addition to a fundamental understanding of the aging vocal mechanism, careful consideration of several factors is important to implementation, including learning environment, schedule and duration of lessons, and physical location. All can affect the outcome of voice training for the older adult. Measures to reduce fatigue, increase concentration, and effectively structure rehearsals also are part of these considerations. Mental and physical fatigue is minimized by using bright lights and music that is printed in an appropriate font size, which will decrease eye strain and allow for better concentration. Also, several breaks during a long rehearsal or voice class can provide necessary time for older adults to restore energy levels.

The scheduling of lessons or classes also can have an impact on vocal output. Concentration levels are highest for older adults during the daytime, so providing opportunities for rehearsal during this period should be beneficial (Lenz 90). One-on-one lessons easily can be scheduled during times when individual students are most alert and focused. Continuity of subject matter also is part of careful planning and scheduling. For example, the synergistic effect of lessons or classes that continue discussions of technique that began in choir rehearsal enhances learning for the older adult. In collaborative efforts with voice teachers, this should not be difficult to achieve. Concepts from the larger rehearsal will be shared in voice class or studio lessons. Learning experiences are linked; the student experiences the fulfillment of a need, such as improvement in breathing for a phrase in a "Messiah" chorus. Studio teachers might need to spend more time conversing with students to establish those concepts that are needed to foster this kind of continuity. Calendar considerations also have an impact on continuity. For example, rehearsals or lessons scheduled according to a school calendar might not best serve the learning objectives of a non-academic population.

The location of rehearsals can be a contributing factor in an aging singer's demonstrated commitment to an ensemble or lessons. For example, there will be fewer impediments to attendance if rehearsals or lessons can be scheduled in places where public transportation is readily available. It also might be possible to organize carpools for those who are not comfortable driving, which has occurred several times with singers in my voice class. Remember George? Some of the other singers help with his transportation, allowing him to maintain his activity in voice class and in his church choir. In addition, accessible facilities often are necessary for older adults (and others!). Any steps that minimize fatigue and make attendance easier are beneficial and will lead to better results.

Beyond these considerations of environment, schedule, duration, and location, instructors should be sure to make the learning activity purposeful. Older adult learners are no different from anyone else: they do not want to waste time! (Lenz 26, 72). They also want their prior knowledge to be recognized, so introducing new information by establishing connections with prior learning is effective and demonstrates the value placed on their knowledge and experience. Other basic ideas such as starting and ending on time, having a careful plan for discussion or activity, and being well-prepared in your lesson plans are effective methods for teaching adult learners.

In our efforts to meet student needs, we also must remember that there are individual differences among older adults. People do not age at the same rate; therefore, age-related changes are not necessarily the same for everyone. Forgetting to value individual differences is one way to decrease the efficacy of your teaching methods and learning environment (Lenz 89).

**First Encounters and Following Up**

While initial efforts to get to know your singers during the first classes or lessons can seem daunting, the impact of those efforts can have long-lasting positive effects on music making. Advance planning and implementation of methods to make personal connections with the singers are essential elements of this process. These connections not only establish a record of singer abilities for the conductor or voice teacher, but also demonstrate to singers that they are valued for their experience, knowledge, and commitment.

Choir directors and voice teachers can use similar methods of information gathering to establish connections with singers, but the number of resources available to these vocal practitioners will dictate the process to some extent. Both can use an initial interview and/or audition to establish a singer's motivation, experience, attitude about singing, and goals. Questions to be asked during the interview/audition might include:
- Why are you interested in joining this choir (or taking voice lessons)?
- What is your previous experience with singing?
- What do you think is good about your voice?
- Are there areas in your singing that need improvement?
- What do you hope to achieve by being involved in this activity?

If it is possible to meet with singers periodically, the practitioner can ask if they notice any improvements in their singing over recent months, and if they are experiencing any difficulty with singing that they did not have before. These questions, whether written or verbal, provide the framework for knowing each singer as an individual and understanding any developmental changes that are being experienced. The practitioner then can tailor lessons or rehearsals to meet these needs effectively.

Time constraints and numbers of singers can limit the ability of vocal practitioners to address specific needs in the choir rehearsal. But informal meeting times also can be effective for establishing relationships and rapport. Time before and after rehearsals, lessons, or class can provide ample opportunities for this. Many teachers and directors already are familiar with establishing a routine for a rehearsal or lesson; what is less well-known is how to conduct a voice class.

During the first meeting of a voice class, it is important to establish routines. Teachers should come prepared with notebooks, songbooks (with accompaniment CDs if possible), an attendance and payment checklist that gathers names, contact information, and handouts containing class policies regarding attendance and payment. Information about parking sometimes is important as well. All of these steps put students at ease and recognize their needs. The teacher is able to establish a caring atmosphere before he even begins teaching.

When the class starts, an open and inviting atmosphere puts singers at ease and allows them to take risks in front of their peers. This can occur initially by using "ice breakers" and games to get to know each student. Games that focus on spontaneous vocalization, like passing an imaginary noisy object from person to person, are good examples. Sharing your goals for students also is helpful because it reassures them of your expectations; you want them to be committed students, not professionals. Your attitude lowers their perception of risk.

I have found that the next step is to use a significant amount of time for vocalization and explaining technical vocal concepts. During these periods, it can be effective to use props to help explain your points. I have used exercise balls to help students feel the effects of posture. This is done by having students sit on a ball and try to first arch their backs and then slouch their shoulders; they will feel the ball move each time. Sitting with proper upper body alignment minimizes this movement and allows them to focus on their physical sensations. A Slinky® toy can help to describe sound waves and resonance. Have two students stand opposite each other holding the ends of the Slinky, and then direct one to flick a finger against it and note the disturbance that travels along the its entire length. This is similar to the motion of sound waves. I have used scarves to illustrate breath energy. Students hold one end of the scarf and sing while I pull the other end, using the energy with which I want them to sing. These props help students to visualize concepts that can sometimes be abstract or illusive. They can involve more than one student at once, which is effective during a class teaching situation. The remaining class time can be used to choose songs, sing through some as a group and plan for the next class. Subsequent classes can make use of the same vocalization, lecture/song approach.

**Following Up**

Once the teacher has established a pattern of working during each class, it is useful to check in with students about how they have applied what they've learned over the course of a week's participation in other musical activities. Have they practiced their breathing or posture concepts in choir? Have they vocalized anywhere other than in the car on the way to class? Are they having problems implementing anything you've taught them? In many ways, the voice teacher or director functions like a tutor for singing, guiding students through concepts so they can apply proper techniques as they participate in music-making during the rest of their lives. The equation of *targeted vocalises* plus *song literature* plus *answering technical questions* equals *satisfied and successful students*, and is the best way to maximize one's impact on the pupils in a voice class.

**Conclusion**

Working with older singers is not an entirely different experience, but there are important things to remember when teaching this special population. An understanding and willingness to work with the changes in mind and body that older adults encounter is essential. Committing to this understanding is no small task, but proves worthwhile when singers remain dedicated to musical pursuits and are buoyed by their participation in an artistic endeavor. For teachers, there can be no greater satisfaction than supporting lifelong learning through participation in music.

## Works Cited

Ahmad, Nadir and Michael Seidman, "Tinnitus in the Older Adult: Epidemiology, Pathophysiology and Treatment Options" *Drugs Aging* 21.5 (2004): 297-305

Armstrong, D. "Adult Learners of Low Educational Attainment: The Self-Concepts, Backgrounds, and Educative Behavior of Average and High Learning Adults of Low Educational Attainment" Diss. U of Toronto, 1971

Awan, Shaheen N. "The aging female voice; acoustic and respiratory data." *Critical Linguistics & Phonetics.* 20 (2/3): 2006. 171-180

Brandtstädter, Jochen. "Sources of Resilience: Toward Integrating Perspectives" Ed. Thomas M. Hess, and Fredda Blanchard-Felds. *Social Cognition and Aging.* San Diego: Academic Press, 1999. 123-141.

Berk, Laura E. *Development Through the Lifespan*, New York: Pearson Education Inc, 2007

Cross, K. Patricia. *Adults as Learners: Increasing Participation and Facilitating Learning.* San Francisco: Josey-Boss, 1981

Davis, Dolly Caywood. "A Study of the effects of two kinds of vocal exercises on selected parameters in the singing voices of women over age fifty." Diss. U of Iowa. 2000

Erber, Joan T and Irene G Prager, "Age and Memory: Perceptions of Forgetful Young and Older Adults" *Social Cognition and Aging.* Ed. Thomas M. Hess, and Fredda Blanchard-Felds. San Diego: Academic Press, 1999), 197-217

Harvard Women's Health Watch. "Hearing Loss" 6. 6 (1999): 4-6

Ed. Hirano, Minoru, P. H. Dejonckere, Johan Sundberg. *Vibrato*. San Diego: Singular, 1995

Huang, Qi and Jianguo Tang. "Age-related hearing loss or presbycusis." *European Archives of Oto-Rhino-Laryngology*; 267.8 (2010): 1179-1191

Hull, Raymond H. and Stacy R. Kerschen. "The Influence of Cardiovascular Health on Peripheral and Central Auditory Function in Adults: A Research Review" *American Journal of Audiology* 19 (2010): 9-16

Lenz, Elinor. *The Art of Teaching Adults*, New York: CBS College Publishing, 1982

National Institute of Health Senior Health. "Hearing Loss."
<www.nihseniorhealth.gov/hearingloss/hearinglossdefined/01.html>

Sataloff, Robert T. "The Aging Voice", *The NATS Bulletin,* 43 (1987): 20-21

---. ed. *Vocal Health and Pedagogy,* San Diego: Singular, 1998.
    Isenberger, H, Brown, WS, Rothman, H. "Effects of menstruation on the singing voice.
    Part II: further developments in research." Transcripts from the Twelfth Symposium: Care
    Of the Professional Voice. New York NY: The Voice Foundation; 1983:117-123

Sataloff, Robert T. and Brenda Smith, *Choral Pedagogy*. San Diego: Plural Publishing, 2006)

Seashore, Carl E. ed. *Psychology of the Vibrato in Voice and Instrument: Studies in the Psychology of Music.* Iowa City: The University Press, 1936

Singing Mastermind. 19 July 2010 www.singingmastermind.com/category/how-your-voice-works/

US Bureau of the Census; National Institute on Aging, U.S. Department of Commerce, Economics and Statistics Administration. *Aging in the United States: Past, Present, and Future.* 1990. 19 July 2010 <www.census.gov/ipc/prod/97agewc.pdf>

Ware, Clifton. *Basics of Vocal Pedagogy: The Foundations and Process of Singing.* Boston: McGraw-Hill, 1998

# Index

**Age related changes**
   cognitive, 203
   isolation and depression, 204
   ossification, 10, 204
   physiologic, 203
   psychosocial, ii, 203
   retention, 205, 207
   social and personal roles, 204
aging singer, i, ii, 11, 15, 202, 203, 204, 208, 210, 211, 212, 213
**Articulation**, 1, 18, 19
   tongue and jaw, 3, 4, 11, 12, 18, 19, 20
   velum (soft palate), 18
associative memory, 205
cognitive, ii
collaboration, 212
**Coping mechanisms**, 204, 207, 208, 209
   assimilative, accomodative, immunizing mode, 208
Explorers, 203, 206
fundamental frequency, 10, 13
Groupies, 202
**Hearing**, 20, 216
   basilar membrane, 21, 22
   cochlea, 21, 22, 23
   cochlear nerve, 21
   external ear, 20, 21
   hearing pathway, 20
   middle ear, 21
   ossicles (malleus, incus, stapes), 21
   presbycusis, 21
   stereocilia, 21
   tinnitus, 22, 23
Larynx
   arytenoid cartilage, 7
   cricoid cartilage, 7
   epiglottis, 7
   epithelium, 8
   glottis, 8, 9, 14
   hyoid bone, 7
   lamina propria, 8
   phonation, 1, 7, 13
   thyroid cartilage, 7
   vocal folds (vocal cords), 7, 8, 9, 10, 12
   vocal ligament, 8, 9
learning, 206
Lifers, 202, 206
phonation, 2, 4, 7, 9, 11, 13, 15, 18
physiological aging, 24
**recruitment**, 212
resonation, 1, 14
**Respiration**, 1, 4
   bronchi, 1
   bronchioles, 1
   diaphragm, 1, 2
   lungs, i, 1, 2, 9, 14
   residual volume, 2
   trachea, 1, 7
   vital capacity, 2
retention of information, 207
Self-Assessment, 209
**Singing lessons**
   choir, 211
   environment, schedule, duration, 213
   one-on-one, 210
   other options, 212
   voice class, 210, 214
tessitura, 10
timbre, 8
vibrato, i, 8, 11, 12, 202
vocal fold bowing, 9
vocal function exercises, 24
Wounded Warbler, 202
xerostomia, 19

**Sangeetha Rayapati**, DMA, is Associate Professor of Music at Augustana College in Rock Island, Illinois, where she teaches voice and music courses, and coordinates offerings of the Barbara Shellhouse Center for Singing. Over the last decade she has taught singers of all ages, both in the studio and in voice classes, and been recognized through presentations and publications by the International Congress of Voice Teachers, the National Association of Teachers of Singing, the Music Educators National Conference, the American Choral Director's Association, and the College Music Society for her work on voice training and the older adult. She holds undergraduate degrees in Music and Nursing from Valparaiso University and graduate degrees in Vocal Performance with a Certificate in Vocal Pedagogy from the University of Minnesota, where she studied with Dr. Clifton Ware, author of the widely-used textbooks *Adventures in Singing* and *Basics of Vocal Pedagogy*.

In addition to teaching, Dr. Rayapati performs regionally as soloist in opera and oratorio and is a frequent recitalist and collaborator with contemporary composers, most recently recording "Luna, Luna" by William Campbell for the Latino Dance Project. She enjoys illuminating the communicative process of singing for herself and for her students, regardless of age.